Summary of Contents

CREATE STUNNING HTML EMAIL

THAT JUST WORKS!

BY **MATHEW PATTERSON**

Create Stunning HTML Email That Just Works!

by Mathew Patterson

Copyright © 2010 SitePoint Pty. Ltd.

Program Director: Andrew Tetlaw

Technical Editor: Louis Simoneau

Chief Technical Officer: Kevin Yank

Indexer: Fred Brown

Editor: Kelly Steele

Cover Design: Alex Walker

Additional Research: Georgina Laidlaw

Printing History:

First Edition: April 2010

Published by SitePoint Pty. Ltd.

48 Cambridge Street, Collingwood
VIC 3066 Australia
Web: www.sitepoint.com
Email: business@sitepoint.com

ISBN 978-0-9805768-6-3
Printed and bound in Canada

About Mathew Patterson

Active on the Web since GeoCities was cutting edge and the horizontal rule was king, Mathew Patterson has worked as a web designer for companies that include the Australian Stock Exchange and Priceline Europe, in addition to freelancing and contracting in Australia and the UK.

Currently Mathew looks after all the customers for Campaign Monitor, the popular email newsletter web application, where he's involved in writing, community management, and intense table tennis sessions. Since joining Campaign Monitor, Mathew has spoken at conferences in Australia and the US about HTML email and the role of web designers, and once famously had a public disagreement with Jeffrey Zeldman about whether email should actually be designed.

Based just outside of Sydney with his wife and son, Mathew has reviewed more email newsletters than you could possibly imagine, including a surprising number that feature alpacas. Find out more (except about the alpacas) at http://mrpatto.com.

About the Technical Editor

Louis Simoneau joined SitePoint in 2009, after traveling from his native Montréal to Calgary, Taipei, and finally Melbourne. He now gets to spend his days learning about cool web technologies, an activity that had previously been relegated to nights and weekends. He enjoys hip-hop, spicy food, and all things geeky. His online home is http://louissimoneau.com, and his latest project is http://isitgoingtobeok.com/.

About the Chief Technical Officer

As Chief Technical Officer for SitePoint, Kevin Yank keeps abreast of all that is new and exciting in web technology. Best known for his book, *Build Your Own Database Driven Web Site Using PHP & MySQL*, he also co-authored *Simply JavaScript* with Cameron Adams and *Everything You Know About CSS Is Wrong!* with Rachel Andrew. In addition, Kevin hosts the *SitePoint Podcast* and co-writes the *SitePoint Tech Times*, a free email newsletter that goes out to over 240,000 subscribers worldwide.

Kevin lives in Melbourne, Australia and enjoys speaking at conferences, as well as visiting friends and family in Canada. He's also passionate about performing improvised comedy theater with Impro Melbourne (http://www.impromelbourne.com.au/) and flying light aircraft. Kevin's personal blog is *Yes, I'm Canadian* (http://yesimcanadian.com/).

About SitePoint

SitePoint specializes in publishing fun, practical, and easy-to-understand content for Web professionals. Visit http://www.sitepoint.com/ to access our blogs, books, newsletters, articles, and community forums.

To my wife Beth, for her love, support, and remarkable ability to feign interest in the nerdiest of topics, and to our beautiful son Sam. Thank you both.

—Mathew

Table of Contents

Chapter 5   Understanding Permission <span></span>

Foreword

For a lot of designers, the job ends the moment the site launches. You've polished the design, built the CMS, and the happy client's check is in the mail. Next, please.

Unfortunately, there's a big opportunity being missed here.

Launching a great website is one thing. But as a designer, you can also play a key role in ensuring that website achieves the actual goals for which it was designed. As well as leading to a more satisfied client, it can provide an additional revenue stream for your business and help set you apart from your competition.

Whether your client's goal is to sell widgets, drive membership, or build a passionate audience, email marketing (done correctly) is one of the most effective ways to achieve it. It's that "done correctly" bit that is often overlooked, and it makes all the difference in the world.

When we launched Campaign Monitor in 2004, email marketing truly was a dark art. Tips on designing emails, getting them delivered, and offering the service to your clients were nonexistent. Since that time, we've spent countless hours researching the best way for designers to plan, design, and build email marketing programs that achieve the best results possible for their clients.

For the first time ever, all of this research and experience has been collated, updated, and refined into a single resource. Not only will you learn how to offer results-driven email marketing to your clients, you'll also find practical tips on selling this service to your clients and creating a passive income stream for your design business. And who isn't interested in doing that?

Dave Greiner, Campaign Monitor co-founder

Preface

How do you feel when your clients ask you to create an email newsletter design? I've witnessed two common reactions from web designers I've spoken to:

- HTML email is evil. It should never be used, and I feel a little ill for even hearing the words spoken.

- HTML email doesn't really work; the designs never look like they're meant to.

In the business world, on the other hand, people neither know about nor care about "HTML email"; they just want a nice-looking email newsletter that drives people to open it and read, click, or buy.

This book is for web designers who are looking for a way to design and build effective HTML emails for their clients or bosses. In the following chapters, we'll cover how to plan, design, and build HTML emails that produce real results.

Why should you trust me to tell you about it? Well, I'm a web designer too, and these days I'm part of the Campaign Monitor team, where we spend all day researching and reading some terrific email newsletters. I can tell you without a doubt that it's possible to produce truly excellent emails that work whether read using Gmail or Pine (a text-based email client that had its heyday in the early nineties).

My goal is for you to reach the end of this book with all the skills and information you need to be able to confidently offer your clients email newsletter design that they'll be happy to pay for. Let's get started!

Who Should Read This Book

This book is aimed at front-end web designers looking to expand the range of services they offer their clients to include HTML email. You should already have at least intermediate knowledge of HTML and CSS, as we'll be applying those skills to the slightly different medium of HTML email.

What's in This Book

By the end of this book, you'll be able to take your HTML and CSS skills and deploy them to build beautiful, effective, and compatible HTML emails. You'll also have a good idea of how to communicate with your clients about their email campaigns, and how to integrate email services into your or your company's offerings.

This book comprises the following six chapters. Read them in order from beginning to end to gain a complete understanding of the subject, or skip around if you only need a refresher on a particular topic.

Chapter 1: *Why Email?*

Before we dive into learning all the ins and outs of HTML email, we'll have a quick look at why email is important, and why it should be part of your web design arsenal. With any luck, I'll succeed in convincing you that, far from being a dark art practiced only by unscrupulous marketers, the design and construction of HTML email is a core part of designing for the Web.

Chapter 2: *Planning an Email Campaign*

As with any kind of design, the most important work happens before you even turn on your computer or pull out your sketch paper and pencils. This chapter covers how to discuss a new project with your client to gain all the information you need beforehand, and how to formulate a clear plan that will let you proceed with designing and building an effective HTML email campaign, hassle-free.

Chapter 3: *Design for the Inbox*

This is where the real fun starts. With a clear plan in hand, we can now set about the task of designing our email. In this chapter, you'll learn the key ways in which design for the inbox differs from design for the browser, and how to embrace this new set of constraints. Everything you take for granted in the web design world—from layout, to imagery, to typography—needs to be re-evaluated when designing HTML emails, and this chapter is your guidebook to that exotic new land.

Chapter 4: *Coding your Emails*

HTML in email is exactly the same as HTML in web pages—in 1999. While browsers have leaped ahead in CSS support in recent years, email clients have stagnated or, worse, regressed. You'll need to dig out your table-based layout techniques from your bottom drawer, hold your nose, and dive in. Fortunately, this chapter will give you the lowdown on which CSS selectors and properties, as well as which other technologies, are available to you in the current crop of email software. You'll also learn the key tips and tricks to achieving reliable, compatible layout with a minimum of tears.

Chapter 5: *Understanding Permission*

Unlike web pages, which are generally only loaded when a browser user chooses to do so, HTML emails often arrive unbidden. As a consequence, they often meet with a less than favorable response from many readers. What's more, they're also regulated by a number of laws that vary between countries. In this chapter, we'll explain the best ways of dealing with the issue of permission, to keep your recipients happy and your clients on the right side of the law.

Chapter 6: *Selling Email to Your Clients*

All the skills you've learned throughout the book amount to nothing if you're unable to convince your client to pay for them. But we thought of that. So that's why there's a whole chapter on how to present your new skills, integrate them into your service offers, and make your clients realize that email is a huge, untapped market where you can help them gain the jump on their competitors.

Where to Find Help

SitePoint has a thriving community of web designers and developers ready and waiting to help you out if you run into trouble. We also maintain a list of known errata for this book, which you can consult for the latest updates; the details follow.

The SitePoint Forums

The SitePoint Forums[1] are discussion forums where you can ask questions about anything related to web development. You may, of course, answer questions too. That's how a discussion forum site works—some people ask, some people answer, and most people do a bit of both. Sharing your knowledge benefits others and strengthens the community. A lot of interesting and experienced web designers and developers hang out there. It's a good way to learn new stuff, have questions answered in a hurry, and have a blast.

The Book's Website

Located at http://www.sitepoint.com/books/htmlemail1/, the website that supports this book will give you access to the following facilities:

The Code Archive

As you progress through this book, you'll note a number of references to the code archive. This is a downloadable ZIP archive that contains every line of example source code that's printed in this book, as well as other supporting documents. If you want to cheat (or save yourself from carpal tunnel syndrome), go ahead and download the archive.[2]

Updates and Errata

No book is perfect, and we expect that watchful readers will be able to spot at least one or two mistakes before the end of this one. The Errata page[3] on the book's website will always have the latest information about known typographical and code errors.

The SitePoint Newsletters

In addition to books like this one, SitePoint publishes free email newsletters, such as the *SitePoint Tech Times*, *SitePoint Tribune*, and *SitePoint Design View*, to name a few. In them, you'll read about the latest news, product releases, trends, tips, and

---

[1] http://www.sitepoint.com/forums/
[2] http://www.sitepoint.com/books/htmlemail1/code.php
[3] http://www.sitepoint.com/books/htmlemail1/errata.php

techniques for all aspects of web development. Sign up to one or more SitePoint newsletters at http://www.sitepoint.com/newsletter/.

The SitePoint Podcast

Join the SitePoint Podcast team for news, interviews, opinion, and fresh thinking for web developers and designers. We discuss the latest web industry topics, present guest speakers, and interview some of the best minds in the industry. You can catch up on the latest and previous podcasts at http://www.sitepoint.com/podcast/, or subscribe via iTunes.

Your Feedback

If you're unable to find an answer through the forums, or if you wish to contact us for any other reason, the best place to write is books@sitepoint.com. We have a well-staffed email support system set up to track your inquiries, and if our support team members are unable to answer your question, they'll send it straight to us. Suggestions for improvements, as well as notices of any mistakes you may find, are especially welcome.

Acknowledgments

Making this book possible were Jarrod Taylor (the ultimate modern henchman), Dave Greiner, and Mark Wyner for their email research, and Ros Hodgekiss for her design gallery work. I gratefully thank them all. Thanks also to the Campaign Monitor support team who bore the load for me, and to my wonderful wife and son who now know far more about HTML email than they ever wanted.

Conventions Used in This Book

You'll notice that we've used certain typographic and layout styles throughout the book to signify different types of information. Look out for the following items:

Code Samples

Code in this book will be displayed using a fixed-width font, like so:

```
<h1>A Perfect Summer's Day</h1>
<p>It was a lovely day for a walk in the park. The birds
were singing and the kids were all back at school.</p>
```

If the code is to be found in the book's code archive, the name of the file will appear at the top of the program listing, like this:

example.css

```
.footer {
  background-color: #CCC;
  border-top: 1px solid #333;
}
```

If only part of the file is displayed, this is indicated by the word *excerpt*:

example.css *(excerpt)*

```
  border-top: 1px solid #333;
```

If additional code is to be inserted into an existing example, the new code will be displayed in bold:

```
function animate() {
  new_variable = "Hello";
}
```

Where existing code is required for context, rather than repeat all the code, a vertical ellipsis will be displayed:

```
function animate() {
    ⋮
    return new_variable;
}
```

Some lines of code are intended to be entered on one line, but we've had to wrap them because of page constraints. A ➥ indicates a line break that exists for formatting purposes only, and should be ignored:

```
URL.open("http://www.sitepoint.com/blogs/2007/05/28/user-style-she
➥ets-come-of-age/");
```

Tips, Notes, and Warnings

Hey, You!

Tips will give you helpful little pointers.

Ahem, Excuse Me ...

Notes are useful asides that are related—but not critical—to the topic at hand. Think of them as extra tidbits of information.

Make Sure You Always ...

... pay attention to these important points.

Watch Out!

Warnings will highlight any gotchas that are likely to trip you up along the way.

Chapter 1

Why Email?

Email has been around forever, it seems. In this age of shiny web applications and mobile computing, is there still a role for email? If there is, how and why should web designers be a part of that?

Email: The Heart of the Internet

When Oprah has one million Twitter followers, and your mother is waiting for you to accept her friend request on Facebook, surely we are officially in the age of Web 2.0? Perhaps not. December 2009 research in the US shows that less than half of all internet users are involved in online social networks.[1]

The same study showed that 89% of those same internet users are sending or reading email, the highest percentage of the study.

Whether at work or home, almost everyone who's on the Internet at all is using email, and there are no signs of that number declining. Certainly some activities—like photo sharing and status updates—that used to occur via email are now separated

---

[1] http://www.pewinternet.org/Trend-Data/Online-Activites-Total.aspx

out into other applications, but email still remains the one online communication tool that everyone understands.

Where websites rely on you visiting them, email comes right to your inbox, and because of this it feels somehow more important and personal. Businesses everywhere know this, and so a relatively small but outperforming email marketing industry has grown. Wait, don't panic! Email marketing is a lot more than mail-order brides and genuine replica watches.

Every day, millions of businesses—from sole traders to multinationals—send email to their clients, subscribers, suppliers, and partners. Commercial email returned a whopping $43.62 for every dollar spent on it in 2009, according to the Direct Marketing Association's Power of Direct economic-impact study.[2] With email marketing still providing the highest return on investment of any form of marketing, it's safe to say that email will be around for a long time to come.

In 2010, with the world still recovering from a global financial scare, email is a low-cost, high-return medium that appeals to businesses. For web designers, there's the opportunity to add email design to their services and give clients another way to reach their goals.

Email's Undeserved Bad Rap

Email, especially HTML email, receives a bad rap in general, especially from web designers. For some, it has become a synonym for spam, thanks to the very real problem of mass unsolicited sending. Email done right, on the other hand, is a powerful tool that can produce real value for both the sender and recipient.

Jeanne S. Jennings, in her email marketing bible, *The Email Marketing Kit* (Melbourne: SitePoint, 2007), provides one of the best summaries on the benefits of email marketing. I've paraphrased it here:

- Email is *cost-effective.* While there are costs involved in email marketing, such as copywriting and design, your production and delivery costs are significantly cheaper than that of direct mail. For the same amount, you can send out around a hundred emails for every direct mail letter.

---

[2] http://directmag.com/magilla/1020-e-mail-roi-still-slipping/

Email *builds relationships*. While email may not be the only method that helps connect you with your audience, it's the least intrusive—enabling the recipient to respond at their leisure. A well thought-out email plan can create and strengthen customer loyalty.

Email is *active*. Email marketing actively sends your message to interested people, rather than relying on them to find you each time.

Email provides *timely results*. The time between distribution and delivery of an email marketing campaign can be measured in minutes rather than days. This allows you to choose the time you deliver your messages with more precision, and also means results will become evident quickly after you start your campaign.

Email is *quick to produce*. Once you're set up to run email campaigns, you can easily launch a major marketing initiative to all your customers in a few hours. There's no other direct marketing source that could be implemented in this sort of time period.

Email *accommodates hyperlinks*. With just a click of the mouse, a customer can go from reading your marketing message to purchasing at your online checkout. This speedy one-step process is what marketing dreams are made of.

Email provides *detailed feedback*. Email marketing allows for comprehensive feedback. You can measure how many of your emails were successfully delivered and opened, how many times your links were clicked on, and, importantly, how many sales you made. This also enables thorough campaign analysis.

Email enables *affordable segmentation and targeting*. Email marketing is agile, allowing you to vary the content sent to customers on your distribution list. You can **segment**, that is, split your lists based on market segments such as geographic location, purchase history, gender, and age to send tailored messages, improving your conversion rate.

Email *plays well with others*. Email works well when part of an integrated direct marketing campaign. While other methods can come across as disruptive or pushy, email is able to prepare your customers for a sales call—or as a follow-up to a face-to-face sale—without getting in a customer's face.

The Different Types of Email Communication

Email itself has limitless uses, and email marketing is more than just sending out an email with a special deal on a product. There are a number of approaches your clients can use to engage their audiences, and each type of email communication sent will deliver varied benefits, and require different design and planning processes. Let's take a closer look at all of them. In specific industries there may be subcategories within each of the broad groupings I've outlined here, but these are the common email types you're likely to be asked to design.

Email Newsletters

As a basis for an ongoing business relationship, there's nothing better than an email newsletter providing reliable, regularly delivered, quality information on relevant and interesting topics. By their very nature, newsletters are sent regularly. A company will usually set a schedule to mail subscribers weekly, every two weeks, or monthly, enabling the company to regularly promote its news and events in a timely way.

Email newsletters are widely used. They're a common, proven communications tool that help countless organizations achieve their brand awareness, customer retention, ad revenue, and other goals. While a client may yet be be at the stage to compile enough content for a subscriber list on a regular basis, very few of your clients are unlikely to see the business benefits of email newsletters. If they don't want to start one just yet, they're likely to reconsider in the not-too-distant future.

Catalog Emails

Catalog emails are the electronic newsletters of the online retailer. Where a service organization might send an email newsletter, a company that sells products may prefer mailing an electronic catalog to subscribers on a regular basis.

Depending on the retailer, the catalog can contain the same sections each time, or each issue might vary from the last. In building a catalog email, you should agree on a set number of items to include in each issue, as you would in an email newsletter. This will keep the preparation of the creative as straightforward as possible each time, while keeping your client's email budget on track. Bear in mind though that laying out catalogs can be more finicky, time-consuming work than producing a simple electronic newsletter.

Announcement Emails

Announcement emails are usually commissioned and produced on an ad hoc basis, when the client has time-critical information to tell their subscribers. Perhaps your client has a limited-time offer that they want to promote. They might have been invited at the last minute to speak at a conference or industry event, and want to encourage clients to attend. A host of possibilities can spark the need to send an announcement email.

One-off announcement emails are usually short and contain just one call to action. Often, there'll be minimal lead time for the announcement, so there's a need to turn the job around quickly. If your client believes they're likely to use announcement emails often, you might offer to prepare a suitable template in advance; this will reduce the time it will take to get their announcements out to subscribers.

Press Releases

Although they sound like announcements, press releases are more public relations than sales. Companies from all industries prepare press releases around corporate and governance developments, product or service launches and upgrades, community contribution and involvement, and so on.

Your clients might produce media releases frequently, but they're unlikely to write them on a regular basis—every Monday, for example. In fact, time frames around media release mailing tend to be tight at best, and unpredictable at worst. Again, offering to prepare a media release email template for clients who have active public relations strategies might save time and hassle when it comes to distributing the release. This type is likely to differ from one used to make announcements.

Sales and Sign-up Process Emails

If your clients sell products or services through their websites, they may need to prepare emails that support or augment the purchase process. If they accept any sort of user sign-up through their sites—for a newsletter, for competitions, or even from visitors who want to register their interest in an activity that the company's undertaking—there's the potential for you to add value.

As well as helping your client plan an email sequence, you might design email templates and create landing pages to support the sales or sign-up process. A **landing page** is the first page of a site that a visitor sees after clicking through from an email. Perhaps you'll also set the messages to mail through an email autoresponder, and test the sequences before they're made live. Why not tie in monitoring to help your client assess the success of each email? Although sales process emails may seem cut and dried, you can see there's a lot of scope for designers to show off their skills here.

The Opportunity for Web Designers

Just as the vast majority of websites are rather poorly designed, most commercial emails fail to make good use of the capabilities of plain text or HTML and CSS.

Competition for web design work is immense, but right now there are few web design firms and freelance designers willing to offer HTML email design as part of their service. Many refuse to do it, or will leave their clients to work it out for themselves. As noted designer Jeremy Keith of Clearleft told me, "I've never done an HTML email in my life, and I don't intend to do so."

Since you have at least picked up this book, you are already well ahead of the competition. As you work through the chapters you'll see that it's relatively easy to produce emails that are far better than most of what's being sent out right now. Check out Chapter 6 in particular for the rundown on how to encourage your clients to be really involved in effective email marketing and communication.

So, now that I've outlined *why* you should learn to design and build HTML emails, it's time to dirty our hands with the *how*. As with all design, the first step is to plan, plan, and plan some more.

Planning an Email Campaign

How hard can it be to design and build an HTML email, really? I mean, even my mom can send emails (though she still has some problems with the caps lock key).

Sending emails may be easy, but running an email campaign that delivers the desired results can be a lot more complicated. Using a simple planning process, we can build a solid base from which to design, and save ourselves a lot of time and hassle. In this chapter, we'll go through the all-important planning phase of an email campaign. Then, in Chapter 3, we'll work from that plan to create our email's design.

Planning Is Essential

As designers, we might consider the planning phase to be outside our scope and handled by the client instead. Often a client will have the same opinion, relegating a designer to the technical work and the pretty pictures. Although this is a valid approach, it can lead to a beautifully designed but ineffectual email. That's bad for your client, and for your prospects of future work.

If we can help our clients to create campaigns that actually *work*, they'll be happier, and we can charge more for our services as specialized email campaign consultants. We'll discuss this in more detail in Chapter 6.

If you have ever worked on a website larger than a few pages, you will know how frustrating it is when you've sunk hours of work into the project, only to find out that the client has changed their mind about what the website is actually meant to do. Without a clear plan up front, a website can often end up being a collection of disconnected pages lacking the structure to help visitors make sense of it. An email can suffer exactly the same problems, albeit on a smaller scale.

Of course, we're talking about business, rather than personal, emails here. There's no real planning required to send a photo of your cat to your friend; you just need to remember to actually attach the image. If we want to create a really useful email newsletter, we'll need to do more planning beforehand. What's the purpose of the email? Who are the people it will be sent to, and what are they expecting to receive? What will success look like for this project?

When you're approached to create an HTML email, it will be your job to find answers to these questions before you crack open Photoshop or your favorite text editor. Otherwise, you may end up with a gorgeous, beautifully coded email that's only ever opened by filtering software and cats walking across keyboards.

Rather than just explain how you can apply planning principles to your next project, we'll take a typical client and work through the planning, designing, and coding processes required. I always find that building it for real is a much faster way to learn than just reading the theory.

 In a hurry?

If you bought this book in a desperate rush because your client is demanding an HTML email and you've never built one in your life, substitute your own details with that of your client's in our case study, and we'll walk through each step. In this chapter we'll plan out the email, and in subsequent chapters we'll design, code, and send it.

Meeting Our Client

Today's busy supervillain has no time to do basic death trap maintenance, or deal with the Home Owners Association over concerns that their volcano lair is "not in keeping with the area."

Enter the henchman (or henchperson, if you prefer). Every villain needs at least one henchman to fire inaccurately, put gas in the submarine, and laugh deferentially at all the right moments.

But good henching doesn't just occur by chance, and successful henchpeople need to be on a path of continual improvement. *Modern Henchman* magazine is the journal of choice for the professional henching community.

We've visited them in their decidedly nonsecret lair and chatted about their ideas for a new email newsletter, and they've agreed to work with us to make it happen.

To kick it off, we'll need to answer some basic questions. These questions will be always be more or less the same, whether you're working for a client, an internal team, or your own startup (in the latter case, they're questions you need to be asking *yourself*).

You can find these questions in an editable document included in the book's code archive download, and use them for your own projects.

The *Modern Henchman* Magazine Client Briefing

Who are you sending these emails to?
  - Current subscribers of the print magazine
  - People who sign up on our website
  - Customers who purchased from our site

What is the main reason for sending these emails?
  To increase sales of our Modern Henchman line of products, by encouraging people to buy for the first time and by making readers repeat buyers

What type of emails are you planning to send?
  Customer newsletters

- Subscription reminders
- Invoices and purchase receipts

What type of content do you want to send?

- Special offers
- Informative articles that tie in to our products

How often would you be sending emails?

The newsletter will be sent once a month, with other reminders and notifications as required

Do you have an existing visual design you would like the email to match?

Yes, the website at modernhenchman.com

Do you have examples of other emails that you like?

- Amazon.com product emails
- Apple sales emails

Our client realizes that subscribers with an ongoing connection and past purchasers are the most likely people to purchase from them in the future. Sending an email newsletter or offer to their customers once or twice a month is a very cost-effective way of staying in touch.

It also keeps them in their customers' minds, ensuring that when they need a freeze ray or an exploding hat, modernhenchman.com is their first stop.

Now that we have our client brief, we can start to work out what needs to be done in order to complete the project. The first step is to define in more detail what a successful project will look like.

Setting Goals

Any time you approach a design challenge, you need to have a clear target in mind. This is no less important for an email newsletter than it is for a website or printed matter.

Taking the client's answers from our initial brief, we can restate them in the form of measurable goals. More than just measurable, the goals should also be as specific as possible.

Our client has said they want to increase sales to print subscribers, and convert new customers from email-only subscribers to active customers. That's a good start, but it's wise to try to nail down some more specific goals. For example, what exactly do they mean by "increase sales"? Is it enough to have just one more sale? That might sound ridiculous, but there are some products and services where a single sale could pay for an entire year of email campaigns. Your client may sell consulting services for thousands of dollars per engagement, or they may sell Web 2.0 gradient stickers for a dollar per box. We need to be detailed and specific in order to set useful goals.

Some clients may be uncomfortable giving you specific financial information; they might instead state their goals in terms of the number of visitors arriving at their site from links in the email. If they know that 1.8% of website visits convert into a sale, knowing how many people visit the website from the email can be roughly converted to a dollar value.

Sit down with your client and show them some example goals you have come up with based on their brief. That may lead to follow-up discussion that can help them clarify in their own minds what they want to achieve through their emails. For our client, we might suggest this primary goal: generate at least $400 in sales directly from newsletter subscribers within the first week of each email being sent.

Your client may not have a goal that's directly tied to a financial return. For some businesses, a reply from the reader might be exactly what they want to achieve.

Here are some other examples of goals you could consider:

- Re-establish direct contact with 5 previous clients
- 40% of subscribers open the email
- 20% of subscribers click at least one link
- 30 people visit this specific page on the site

You get the idea. All these goals can be easily measured, so you'll be able to identify when you've achieved them. Sometimes that won't be possible. For example, it may take years for a customer to commit to buying a new warehouse layout system or mainframe installation. The measurable goals in those cases could be about maintaining a relationship, where the measurement is email replies received from the customer.

This process is about more than just producing goals, it is also to encourage our clients—and ourselves as designers—to think carefully about why we are sending the emails in the first place. After all, if the person or company sending the email does not really know the point, the chances of the recipient caring about it are very poor indeed.

Measuring Success

Once we have one or more goals in place, we'll need to set up the tools or processes that will be used to tell if those goals have been met. That might include sales figures from a certain department, reports from your email service provider, or analytics from the website.

If you're using specialized software (whether internal or external) to send the emails, a lot of these measurements may be provided for you as part of the package. The kinds of figures you can expect to be able to track are:

Open rates
How many of the people who received the email actually read it? This number is calculated by monitoring the download of tracking images inside each email. Unfortunately, many email clients don't download images by default, so not every open can be recorded. Similarly, some email clients only show plain text, with no downloaded images.

Click rates
How many of the people who opened the email actually clicked on a link? Typically, email sending services redirect each link through their own tracking service to record those clicks.

Forwards
How many people actually used the "send to a friend" function to forward the email? (Assuming your software has this function.)

Unsubscribes
How many people chose to unsubscribe from further emails using the software's built-in unsubscribe system?

Conversion rate

How many people who clicked through went on to actually buy, or download a trial, or perform another action you can track? Software like Google Analytics can be used to record these actions, and tie them back to particular sources, including your email campaigns.

The most important measurement isn't the raw numbers themselves, but the *change* in these numbers from one campaign to the next (also called the **trend**). After we send each campaign, we'll be making changes to the email content and design, even to the day of the week and time of day that we send. The historical measurements will quickly tell us if our changes are successful or not.

We've reached the point where we have goals for the email campaign, and we know how to tell if we've reached those goals. Only now should we start putting together a plan for the HTML email itself.

Emails are built with the same technologies as web sites: HTML and CSS. However, there are some big differences in what makes an appropriate design for email.

Planning Your Content

It's tempting for web designers to think of HTML email as a little one-page website. After all, it's just HTML and CSS, and a good number of people will be viewing the email in a web browser anyway, right?

That's all true, but websites and emails really are two different media. Just as print designers had to acclimatize to the unique constraints and opportunities of the Web, web designers working with email also need to adjust their thinking.

An Email Is Not a Website

We tend to think of websites as being an online storefront, in that people actively come to our site, whether directly, by searching, or by following a link. When a visitor comes to our website, they normally have some idea already about what they're expecting to find. Visually, the site takes up their full browser window.

An email is a different case. Your inbox is more like your house than a storefront. Emails come to you without you taking any action. When they arrive, the visible area of the email may only be a fraction of the size of a web browser window. Take a look at the typical email software shown in Figure 2.1.

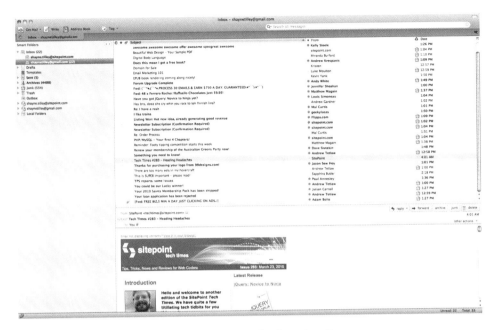

Figure 2.1. Standard email software in action

Notice how busy this window is compared to a web browser? The actual email takes up only a small percentage of space at the bottom, and is surrounded by other items competing for attention. Folders, notes, and other emails fight to be noticed.

So our email is going to have a much harder time being understood than a website displaying the same content. This will affect the way we design our email, and the way we write our content. As designers, we need to be respectful of the fact that our readers (or our client's readers) have let us invade their personal space.

Unless readers are devoted "Inbox Zero" converts, our email will be just another item in a long, long list that's interrupting their real work. We're asking them to pay attention to our email, and usually to take some kind of action. In return, we owe them an email that doesn't take up more time than is necessary, is easy to read, and is actually useful.

Before we dig into the visual aspects of HTML email design, we need to know what content our design is going to be centered around. Every client has their own idea of what should go into an email, and most will have a hugely inflated sense of how important their email is to the people who receive it.

Email in the Real World

Clients have a vision of their readers sitting in their chairs, hitting "Get Mail" every few seconds just to hear the glorious sound of a new email arriving. The reality, as we all know from our own experience, is rarely as positive. To be worthy of more than a cursory glance and a swift trip to the junk mail folder, our email must have immediate, obvious value. This starts with the subject line revealing who the email is from, and what value it offers the recipient.

"Information overload" is a horrible phrase, but we all know what it means. Too much information is given to us, and there's too little time to actually use it. Websites can be content-rich and complex, but at least you can ignore sections of a website.

An email is much more invasive, coming directly to your computer and into your face. While there are no absolute rules, generally our subscribers will be happier with a shorter email than one that tries to pour a website's worth of content into that tiny email pane.

It can be tough to sell this idea to clients. They tend to think that everything they produce is important and interesting to every subscriber. Of course, they're unlikely to treat the emails they *receive* with the same rapt attention they expect for the emails they send—and this might be worth pointing out.

With those general concepts in mind, let's sit down with our client and hash out the content for their newsletter.

Planning the *Modern Henchman* Newsletter

Our client has provided us with this list of content for the *Modern Henchman* newsletter:

- information on the featured product of the month
- teasers for stories in the magazine
- a link to send the email on to a friend
- a featured article

Now we need a way to prioritize this list and narrow it down. A simple way to do this is by asking one more question: "What is the one action you want your reader to take after they read the email?" *Modern Henchman* request that "the reader should click through to learn more about our featured product" when they receive their regular monthly email.

Your client might seek a different preferred action from their readers, such as sending a reply, visiting a certain page, or forwarding on the email. We could go on to select perhaps two or three desired actions. After that, though, we risk having so many possible choices that the reader is paralyzed into taking no action at all.

Now we can rank our content according to what best supports the desired action, and what will most likely meet our overall goals for the email campaigns.

Modern Henchman might end up with a priority list like this:

- information on the featured product of the month (this directly supports our primary action)
- featured article (building our reputation for knowledge)
- link to send the email onto a friend
- teasers for other stories

With this list we can now create an outline for the newsletter, establishing a structure we can carry through from edition to edition. Based on responses from subscribers, we may change this over time, but always keeping our goals clearly in view.

Our final step before we launch into the visual design is to gather all the content for our first email. This can sometimes be a time-consuming task, typically relying on the client to provide material.

For *Modern Henchman*, we can grab a lot of the content for a typical issue from their website, which has the article archive and full product descriptions.

It's Okay to Reuse Content

While you might think that repeating content from the blog or website is a cheat, the reality is that most newsletter subscribers will rarely visit the website unless they're making a specific transaction. The most recent statistics show that more than 90% of internet users still have no understanding of what RSS is, let alone how to use it to keep up with websites.

Even at Campaign Monitor, where customers are mostly internet-savvy web designers, we receive a much bigger response from our email campaigns than from our blog entries. So reusing materials from the website is a smart way to go, and can save a lot of time.

At this stage, we just need representative content that we can build our design around, so creating a dummy sample issue with some content from the website is a good idea.

Lorem Ipsum

I recommend you avoid using *lorem ipsum* text as filler, even though it's common in website design. Too many emails (and too many websites) have been designed using placeholder that turned out being totally different in length, style, and shape from the actual content. The design has then had to be tweaked, well after it should've been finalized.

HTML Email Q&A

Before we move onto designing our email in Chapter 3, we'll go over some common email questions your client may ask, and suggest how to handle them.

How long should an email be?

As short as you can make it, without making it useless. There are some businesses sending very long and complex material in email form, but they're rare. The typical inbox is exceedingly full already, so is an unpleasant space in which to spend time. So get in, get your message across, and get out.

From reviewing many thousands of newsletters for Campaign Monitor, the typical length for a content-heavy newsletter (as opposed to an invitation or simple notice) is two or three screens' worth. That seems reasonable. As always, keep your client's audience in mind, as their needs or expectations may be different.

Should I put the full articles in the email, or just teasers and links to the site?

If shorter is better, linking to the full article online is often the way to go. If you have expansive content, putting it all in the email will be overwhelming. On the other hand, if you can write a shorter version, or carry your point across in a few paragraphs, you could save your reader time by giving them everything they need without having to click through.

How often should I send emails?

As always there is no single answer, but a 2009 survey[1] found that 73% of respondents cited "sending too frequently" as the main reason for opting out of an email mailing list. Conversely, email that's too infrequent risks subscribers forgetting they ever signed up, or finding another solution to the problem you're trying to solve for them.

In general, it's better to err towards too few emails than too many. The answer in any specific case will depend on what the subscribers expect, as well as the timeliness of the content.

But then, you can simply ask your subscribers—and even people who've just unsubscribed—how often they'd prefer to receive your content. Check out a post on this topic on the Campaign Monitor blog.[2]

What is the best time to send?

Endless theories have been proposed and tested about the perfect time to send an email campaign. Studies have been unhelpful, because the mystical perfect day and time seems to shift unpredictably from one study to the next.

---

[1] http://www.merkleinc.com/wmspage.cfm?parm1=919
[2] http://www.campaignmonitor.com/blog/post/3027/changing-email-frequency/

See Email Marketing Reports[3] for some study results and a few ideas that can help you find a suitable starting point.

Of course, you also need to consider your content and your audience; some types of content will lend themselves to a Monday morning arrival, others to a lazy Sunday afternoon. The only really useful answer to this question is, "Try a few different times and see what works best for you."

Is it okay to buy or rent an email list?

Generally, no, it isn't. Although there are services and products that claim to have fully opt-in up-to-date databases, you have no real way of confirming that. Most email service providers and anti-spam systems take a very dim view of purchased email lists. The risk is too high, and the chance of success too low to bother with.

Take the slower approach of building your own opt-in list over time, by interacting with people yourself.

What is a good open rate?

This is yet another question for which there is no simple answer. There is such enormous variation between industries, companies, and recipient lists that overall statistics are unhelpful. Still, we all know clients will ask anyway, so it's good to have some general idea. Broadly, a typical range is 20-40% of the subscriber list. Read more about how open rates are usually measured and what's considered normal for different industries and sectors on the Campaign Monitor website.[4]

Often the real question your client is asking is, "Why don't I have 100% open rates?" so you'll need to discuss their expectations and the reality of email marketing with them.

How many clicks should I expect?

This follows on from the previous question, but is even less likely to have a reliable answer. Email marketing industry reports tend to quote a 2-15% unique clickthrough

---

[3] http://www.email-marketing-reports.com/iland/2009/06/best-day-to-send-email.html
[4] http://help.campaignmonitor.com/topic.aspx?t=89

rate as typical. This means for every 100 people who open your email, less than 15 would typically click a link.

Business to business emails are often at the higher end of that range, and mass market consumer emails the lower. Emails that are targeted and valuable to the recipient can go much higher, of course.

How can I avoid my email being filtered?

Use magic, if possible. Otherwise, you're unfortunately stuck in the land of trial and error. No email service can honestly guarantee your emails will escape filtering, except in very particular circumstances. The vast majority of the time, it's your actual content (subject line, message body) and possibly your "From" address that filters are checking. Your email service provider is unable to control this, so it's largely up to you.

Some topics, such as pharmaceuticals and mortgages, are so heavily targeted by spammers that legitimate senders will always struggle to avoid filters.

The best approach is firstly to avoid highly common spam words (good luck if you ever need to send an email campaign about Viagra!), and then test your email with as many different clients and filters as you can. If your email is filtered in one or two of the tests, but the rest are okay, you're probably fine. If your email is systematically filtered, there could be a broader problem.

In that case, try using one of the email testing services that give spam filter results with reasons why the email failed. Otherwise, cut out half the content and send the rest. If it passes, there could be a problem phrase or word in the half you omitted.

There are no easy solutions to spam filtering, but you need to make your clients aware that even the same email client in two different installations can behave differently. The best you can do is to test, test, test.

Summary

In this chapter, we've seen why it's vital to incorporate a planning phase into any HTML email project, and what that planning entails. We've learned a little bit about how email differs from the broader field of web design, and we'll be delving deeper into that topic in Chapter 3 as we discuss the design considerations that are unique to email.

I hope I've shown you how, by communicating clearly with your clients up front, asking the right questions, and giving them the right information, you can steer your project towards success before you so much as pick up a sketchpad.

In Chapter 3, we'll set about actually designing the *Modern Henchman* newsletter, and along the way we'll learn the peculiarities of HTML email design in a broader sense.

Chapter **3**

Design for the Inbox

Designing an email requires the same HTML and CSS skills you already possess, but requires that you apply them to a different medium and new design context. In this chapter we'll explore the ways in which an email differs from a website, and how that should affect our design.

We'll also look at the design elements that make up a successful HTML email, and uncover the unique constraints of email client software.

Does email really need designing?

Every major email client, from Outlook to Gmail to Apple Mail, is set up by default to send in HTML format, and comes with a bunch of tools and options to format HTML. So if the tools to create and format HTML email are so simple and widely accessible, why would you even want to involve a designer in the first place? Isn't that a bit like your parents demanding a written budget before you buy lunch at the school cafeteria?

In fact, one of the main reasons designers have historically been against the very idea of HTML email is the poor quality of the emails they're used to seeing. You know exactly what I mean: emails that use every font in the drop-down list, with a heavy preference for Comic Sans in 24pt hot pink. The ones with rainbow backgrounds and little animated cats at the bottom.

"Look how ugly they are!" designers proclaim, and promptly vow to never support HTML email. Unfortunately, in the real world, their valiant stand fails to create a turning point; email software manufacturers won't take away their users' cherished fonts and colors. For every designer who refuses to create well-thought-out, appealing emails, there are 24 marketing assistants with access to Microsoft Word and a massive collection of clip-art CDs. Refusing to design HTML emails doesn't stop them being sent, it just ensures that they'll remain hideous eyesores.

So yes, it's actually important to have design input into emails—at least as far as publication-type emails such as newsletters are concerned. We can all be part of the solution to horrible-looking email, instead of just complaining about it. A well designed email is more readable, attractive, and effective at relaying information.

Designing Plain Text Email

Before we launch into a discussion about designing HTML email, I'll briefly touch on the importance of designing plain text email. You don't have to be sending some fancy web-page-in-my-inbox email to benefit from design skills. Even plain text, the base format for written communication, needs to be designed.

Have you ever received plain text newsletters? An excellent example is the Good Experience[1] newsletter (which is well worth subscribing to). Have a look at the screenshot in Figure 3.1.

---

[1] http://goodexperience.com/

```
-------------------- Good Experience - 17 Feb 10 --------------------
                        By Mark Hurst
          Sign up: http://goodexperience.com/newsletter.php
-------------------------------------------------------------------
```

Wednesday, February 17, 2010

- Customer experience is harder than it looks
- 3 new Gel Videos
- For more reading...
- 3 job posts: CA, MA, PA
- How to post a job
- Fun Stuff


```
-------------------------------------------------------------------
    Customer experience is harder than it looks
-------------------------------------------------------------------
```

I have to admit something strange: I'm amused by poorly designed
websites. The worse the better. Much like some people "love to hate"
movie villains, I get a peculiar satisfaction from finding myself
completely lost in an ill-conceived, over-designed, steaming pile of
a website.

And it happens all the time. With a few notable exceptions, almost
any major site, brand, or company I visit online is at least mildly
frustrating - and surprisingly often I find high-profile sites that
are nearly impossible to use from the first page or two, leaving me
astounded at the supreme waste of time and money they represent.

And I love to hate it - the juicy ridiculousness of it all -
millions of dollars poured into something that is so obviously a
wreck. I think I *have* to enjoy it on some level, given my role as
a customer experience consultant; otherwise work would be pretty
difficult (see also: doctors who can't stand the sight of blood).

I'm guessing you've had a similar experience of being frustrated by
a large company's website. You go online to accomplish simple task
X, or shop for product Y, or browse through information Z - and the
site gives you swooping graphics and miniscule text from the
designers, excited (not exciting) promotions from the marketing
team, and features from the geeks that act as grand staircases to
nowhere... but not the thing you were looking for.

At this moment, your reaction is probably similar to mine, those
four well-known words: what were they thinking?!

Figure 3.1. Plain text email formatting example

Notice anything? How about those typographic characters posing as borders? This is a common approach, using asterisks, equal signs, or underscores to simulate the kind of design elements that books and magazines use all the time.

Even print books that are 100% text undergo the design treatment. Typography is well worth studying as a web designer, and there are some excellent resources online from which to start.

Though many maintain that plain text is all you need for an email, a big old block of unformatted text can be very hard to read. Look at what's missing:

- ability to control text size for headings
- ability to emphasize text through bold or italic type
- possibility of using a display font to draw attention to a subtitle
- control over margins and padding to increase clarity and allow the email to be quickly scanned for the most important information

Thoughtful senders use a variety of techniques to work around these limitations, like the character borders above. Ultimately though, these are often little more than clever hacks, using characters differently from what they were designed for in order to improve the readability of a limited medium.

Despite this, it's important to learn how to make plain text email as clear and readable as possible. Even if you're planning to send only HTML emails, you should *always provide a plain text alternative*. Most email newsletter programs will send a multi-part email consisting of both an HTML version and a plain text alternative, so that the recipient's email client can show either according to its capabilities and settings.

Guidelines for a Readable Plain Text Email

- Use lots of whitespace to avoid having a huge gray blob of text. Leave space between paragraphs and after headings, and aim for paragraphs of four to five lines.

- Keep your line width to about 60 characters. This is a comfortable column width to read, and also maintains compatibility with some older systems that can mess up your formatting if you have longer lines.

- Use short URLs wherever possible. Again, longer URLs can break up and become hard to click on, or copy and paste.

- Make your copy easy to scan by dividing it with clear headings.

Figure 3.2 shows another of my favorite plain text emails, from Highrise.

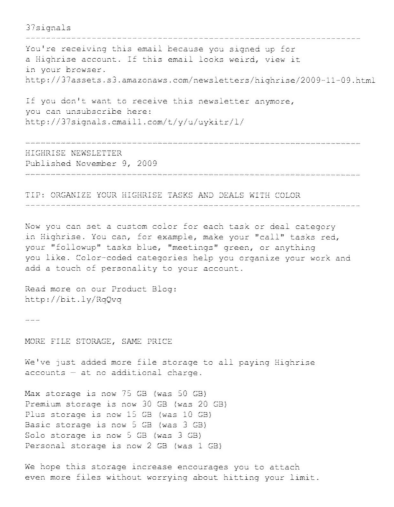

```
37signals
------------------------------------------------------------------
You're receiving this email because you signed up for
a Highrise account. If this email looks weird, view it
in your browser.
http://37assets.s3.amazonaws.com/newsletters/highrise/2009-11-09.html

If you don't want to receive this newsletter anymore,
you can unsubscribe here:
http://37signals.cmail1.com/t/y/u/uykitr/l/


------------------------------------------------------------------
HIGHRISE NEWSLETTER
Published November 9, 2009
------------------------------------------------------------------

TIP: ORGANIZE YOUR HIGHRISE TASKS AND DEALS WITH COLOR
------------------------------------------------------------------

Now you can set a custom color for each task or deal category
in Highrise. You can, for example, make your "call" tasks red,
your "followup" tasks blue, "meetings" green, or anything
you like. Color-coded categories help you organize your work and
add a touch of personality to your account.

Read more on our Product Blog:
http://bit.ly/RqQvq

---

MORE FILE STORAGE, SAME PRICE

We've just added more file storage to all paying Highrise
accounts - at no additional charge.

Max storage is now 75 GB (was 50 GB)
Premium storage is now 30 GB (was 20 GB)
Plus storage is now 15 GB (was 10 GB)
Basic storage is now 5 GB (was 3 GB)
Solo storage is now 5 GB (was 3 GB)
Personal storage is now 2 GB (was 1 GB)

We hope this storage increase encourages you to attach
even more files without worrying about hitting your limit.
```

Figure 3.2. The Highrise newsletter from 37signals

Notice the preheader, which reminds people why they're receiving the email, and the content header, which stands out nicely.

The Plain Text Version of the *Modern Henchman* Newsletter

Our *Modern Henchman* newsletter will have a plain text version; this is to benefit subscribers whose platform (whether legacy or mobile) prevents them from viewing HTML email, or who simply opt for plain text as a personal preference.

Taking the content from our plan in Chapter 2, here's how the plain text version will look:

```
You are receiving this email as a subscriber to Modern Henchman
magazine, or because you signed up at modernhenchman.com


_____


Modern Henchman
_____


In this issue:

* Don't let him get away again!
* Henchman to supervillain?
* Hot Hats for Henchmen
* Lair Maintenance for Beginners


DON'T LET HIM GET AWAY AGAIN!

We uncover the 10 most common tricks superspies use to escape
even the most fearsome of death traps. You'll never let the boss
down again.

Visit http://modernhenchman.com/stories/getaway


_____


HENCHMAN TO SUPERVILLAIN?

Take your henching career to the next level with our easy step-
by-step guide to a brand-new you.

Can you make it?
```

http://modernhenchman.com/stories/henchman2supervillain

HOT HATS FOR HENCHMEN

Stand out from the crowd with this year's selection of henchmen headwear that's both attractive and functional. Available in a range of fashion colors, and perfect for the balding baddy.

Beware, not every head can handle a hat, so take our hat quiz before you buy.

Meet the milliner at
http://modernhenchman.com/stories/hothats

NEVER OUTSHOOT THE BOSS!

Henchman Etiquette Expert Aunty Blake answers your tricky questions about showing up the boss in a fire fight.

http://modernhenchman.com/columns/auntyblake

DIARY OF A HENCHMAN

Finally, the explosive anonymous revelations of a henchman who has worked with some of history's greatest villains. You won't believe what goes on when the giant death ray is turned off.

We have advance copies for every new subscriber to the print version of *Modern Henchman*, so don't delay, subscribe today.

http://modernhenchman.com/subscribe

LAIR MAINTENANCE FOR BEGINNERS

The boss has captured his arch enemy for the third time, but the

```
laser mounts keep slipping off the sharks and the aquarium guy
can't come until Saturday! No need to panic—just follow our simple
illustrated guides and you'll be indispensable.

http://modernhenchman.com/stories/lairmaintenance

     _____



Do your henching colleagues need some tips? Why not send this
email to them.
http://modernhenchman.com/r/l/2AD73FFF/ojlttu/l

If you're not interested in being the best henchman you can be,
please unsubscribe.
http://modernhenchman.com/t/r/u/ojlttu/l/

The Modern Henchman logo and design are trademarks of Hench
International Pty Ltd.
```

Now we have a readable and effective plain text email template that we can use for all our future newsletters. This presents a challenge: if our readers can obtain all the information just fine from this plain text version, why bother with an HTML version?

The Case for HTML Email

Just because we *can* send HTML and CSS in an email doesn't mean we *must*. The fact is that there are some clear benefits to an HTML email, above and beyond the ability to send pictures of cats with English grammar trouble.

Have a glance at the emails shown in Figure 3.3. Here we have the same email in two different formats. Which one jumps out at you more? Which is faster for you to read? What's the most important information in the email?

Figure 3.3. Plain text (left) and HTML (right) versions of the *Good Experience* newsletter

Mark Hurst, the founder and sender of this newsletter, made the decision in March 2010 to send this HTML version as well as the plain text for the first time. He immediately received this comment from a subscriber: "The email is much more pleasant to read and the links are easily visible and inviting."

The HTML version is still mostly text, but it's HTML-rendered text. Look at how much easier it is to spot what the sender considers the key information. Some simple font control and margins create an instant visual hierarchy that plain text struggles to establish. Even the most hardcore anti-HTML email campaigner wouldn't get upset about this. As this illustrates, it's possible to design HTML for email in a way that's actually helpful, and better than the alternative.

Designing HTML Email

If you can agree with me that, in principle, well-designed HTML email is possible, the question we need to answer is, "What does a well-designed HTML email look like?" We're going to try to answer that in the rest of this chapter, and then discover how to build it in Chapter 4.

Along the way, we'll think about how the concepts we're learning can be used to help design an HTML email for *Modern Henchman* magazine.

The Design Environment for Email

Isn't designing an email just like designing a small, one-page web page? Well, yes, in many ways it is. We do use the same design tools and technologies to produce the final result. And the same general design principles are still in play: contrast, repetition, proximity, and alignment are all important.

Any competent web designer already has the capabilities to design an HTML email. There are some important differences, though, and understanding these will make the difference between a tiny web page squished into your inbox, and a valuable and readable email.

If we compare web design to email design, we can come up with a few core distinctions. Let's examine them one by one, and see what lessons we can draw from them.

Your Subscriber May Not Read the Email

The very first element of design that goes into an email isn't strictly "design" at all. It's copywriting. Your email can fly through spam filters like Luke Skywalker in the Death Star trenches and make its way successfully into the inbox, but then remain unopened. This is because, unlike a web page—which visitors can arrive at via links from other pages or search engines—an email is only ever opened when the user *decides* to open it, and often they'll make that decision based on the subject line.

Crafting an appealing and informative subject line is the first step in a successful design. We're unable to make any visual design changes to a subject line, but as designers we should be involved in ensuring that it represents what's in the email, and that it's recognizable and helpful.

If the subject line fails in its job, your beautifully crafted design will never be seen. There's plenty of information out there for help on improving subject lines, as well as research on what makes a subject line succeed or fail.[2]

---

[2] Visit http://www.campaignmonitor.com/blog/post/2546/writing-better-subject-lines/ for some great jumping-off points.

Design Guideline 1: Write a subject line that is …

- informative (mention some of the topics)
- short (or at least has the most important information at the start)
- recognizable (so that it's consistent with other emails from your client)

Looking Through the Rectangular Window

Assuming we've done a decent job with our subject line, our email may be selected from the inbox and displayed in a shortened form. For desktop email clients like Outlook and Apple Mail, the default preview pane is a tiny rectangle of space taking up less than 20% of the screen, as illustrated in Figure 3.4.

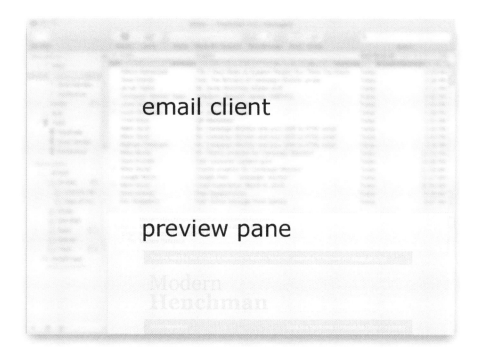

Figure 3.4. Sample screen showing preview pane size

Imagine walking through a mall. Every store has a sign out the front, but all the windows are blacked out except for a square letterbox-sized peephole. To decide whether you want to go inside you need to peek through that slot to see what you can see. That's what the preview pane is like—a limited view of your design and content. For that reason, it's really important that the top of your email is informative.

If all the reader can see is 300 pixels of your background color or an unrecognizable logo, they have to be really keen to bother reading on.

When we come to design our *Modern Henchman* email newsletter, we'll make sure that those first few hundred pixels at the top (and more specifically, the top left) communicate useful information.

Design Guideline 2: Find out what your email looks like in a minimal preview pane.

> What copy is located in the top few hundred pixels of the email? Does it entice people to read on? Is your header too big?

Image Blocking

If you've used any email program that renders HTML, chances are you'll have opened up emails that looked like the one shown in Figure 3.5.

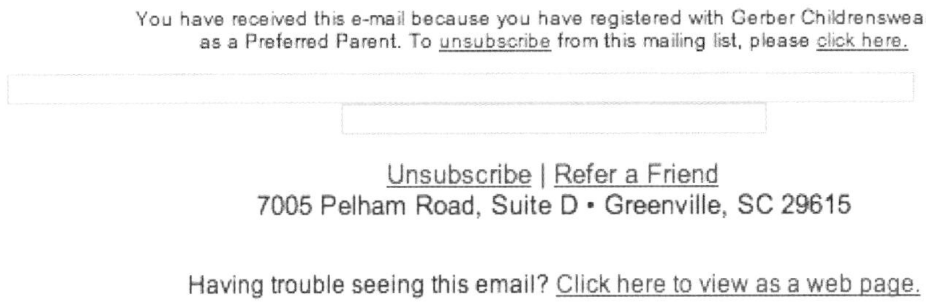

You have received this e-mail because you have registered with Gerber Childrenswear LLC as a Preferred Parent. To unsubscribe from this mailing list, please click here.

Unsubscribe | Refer a Friend
7005 Pelham Road, Suite D • Greenville, SC 29615

Having trouble seeing this email? Click here to view as a web page.

Figure 3.5. All-image email with images blocked

Instead of words or pictures, there's a stack of blocks of various sizes, as if someone is losing a game of Tetris in your inbox. Most of the major email clients, including Outlook, Lotus Notes, and Hotmail, will not display images by default. Instead, they display a broken image icon or an empty rectangle.

The reason image blocking is so common is related to the invasiveness of email that we discussed earlier. When emails arrive without you having taken any action, featuring any content imaginable, it's easy to see how it all can go horribly wrong. Nobody wants to have to explain to their boss why their screen is full of images unsuited to the workplace. To avoid this sort of situation, the email programs insert an extra step in the viewing process to make the reader specifically request to see images.

Email software programs differ in the way they handle images by default, whether using a global setting, or showing images only from your known contacts, or on an individual email-by-email basis. In some cases, embedding the images as MIME-encoded attachments can avoid the image blocking, which is worth knowing. However, sending images as attachments creates a greater risk of being filtered, slower download speeds, and more complex processes. And you can bet that if spammers start embedding all their images as attachments, the email clients will respond and start blocking those as well.

The take-home message for us as email designers is that we cannot simply expect our readers to see the images. Added to that, many readers are unaware that images are missing or how to enable them, so they may just assume the email is meaningless or broken, and throw it out if it contains no content other than images.

So what are we to do? Avoid images entirely? Well, you could, and in many cases a well-formatted HTML email without images can be highly effective and achieve all your goals (see the section called "Almost Image Free" in the Gallery at the end of this chapter for examples of this sort of email). That's not always true, though, and inevitably we'll have clients or bosses who really do have valid requirements for images.

The answer is to always design knowing that your images cannot be relied on. Make sure that if they don't load, the email is still readable and recognizable.

Design Guideline 3: Always check your email with images turned off.
> Does the email still have useful, readable content? Consider especially what the preview pane looks like when there are no images. Do you have visible text in the preview area?

Horizontally Challenged

I remember the momentous time when 800x600 desktop resolutions were finally sufficiently widespread for web designers to move *en masse* to designing websites for this size. We'd been toiling away for years, squeezing websites into 600 measly pixels, so being allowed to stretch out to 760 was like moving from a camp bed up to a queen ensemble.

Unfortunately, I have some bad news. When it comes to email design, you'll need to go down to the garage and drag that camp bed back upstairs, because your emails are probably being read in a very narrow window or frame. Most people don't open emails in a full-screen window; instead, they scroll through a preview pane or viewing column that takes up only a portion of the screen.

Added to that, consider the poor people using mobile email clients who at best have a few hundred pixels with which to work. Web surfers have overcome their fear of scrolling vertically, but horizontal scrolling is still rare. As a result, our email designs will generally be quite narrow, built to work in a limited screen space. Most commercial emails seem to be about 600 pixels wide at the most, which can feel almost claustrophobic when you are used to your 24-inch desktop monitor. This width restriction will naturally lead to certain design styles, such as restricting the number of columns and splitting the elements vertically more than horizontally.

Design Guideline 4: Keep email designs reasonably narrow.
A good maximum width to aim for is 600 pixels.

Essential Elements of an Effective Email

With our design guidelines in hand, we're almost ready to start creating our email. In the same way that nearly all cars have a steering wheel, four wheels, and a dashboard, and that most websites have headers and footers and contact pages, commercial emails tend to share a basic structure.

I've reviewed literally hundreds of thousands of emails over the last few years, and the pattern that emerges is very clear. The elements we will discuss below can be implemented in many ways, but they're almost always present in newsletters and marketing emails. You may not be legally required to have them all, but each one adds to the credibility of your message and the likelihood of it being read.

Permission Reminder

There are many different laws that apply to commercial email according to where you're located in the world. One rule that applies almost everywhere is that you absolutely must have permission to send people bulk email. In most cases, it also makes sense to remind people about how they gave you that permission. We'll be covering this topic in more detail in Chapter 5, but we'll describe it briefly here, as it's an important element that needs to be considered before you start your design.

It's common for people to forget that they signed up, especially if you only send emails rarely, or they only joined because of a competition or special offer. A short message at the top of your email can help people remember, and make them more likely to read on. You may have seen some companies attempt this, but make the reminder infuriatingly vague, such as "You are receiving this because your address was on our list." Well, duh!

Recipients want to know *why* their address is on your list, and how it got there. The more specific you can be, the better. In the case of our *Modern Henchman* newsletter, we know that people are on the list for one of three reasons:

- They bought products from the website recently.
- They filled in the sign-up form on the website.
- They are paying subscribers and this is part of their purchase.

So a simple permission reminder will be something like: "You are receiving this because you are a current subscriber, have bought from us (thanks), or signed up on our website."

Working with your client to write a permission reminder can also be a good way to check that the client *does* have permission to email their list. Seeing the reminder written out plainly can trigger them to say, "Oh, we also added our contact list, Chamber of Commerce members, and local phone directory." Uh-oh.

It's much better to find out *before* you send the email that your client has a very different understanding of permission than you do (or than your email service provider does). You can then work with them to pare the list back to people who are more likely to receive it positively, and who meet your email service provider's rules.

Storing information about how each person signed up (perhaps as a custom data field in your list) can make it simple to create personalized permission reminders. If you know this person bought from you in May this year, you can remind them of that right up front, making them much more likely to respond well to your email.

Panic[3] sent a very attractive and cleverly designed email, shown in Figure 3.6, but it was the addition of the line "You signed up for our list via [product name]" that helped them avoid complaints.

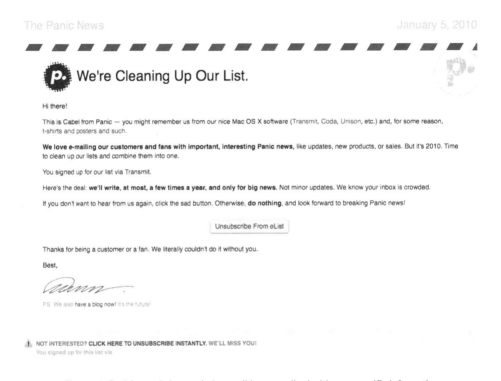

Figure 3.6. Panic's permission reminder email is personalized with user-specific information

Have Recognizable Sender Details

Studies on email open rates have found that trusting the sender is the single most important factor in whether an email is opened or not. That means it's critical to choose an effective and consistent "From" name and email address. You need to choose a name or title that will be recognizable to your readers. Often that will be the company name, or perhaps the product or service people have signed up to learn about.

Some companies have a well-known leader (bgates@microsoft.com), and if your client is among those, you might be able to use their name. Once you've picked an

---

[3] http://www.panic.com/

address, it's important to stick with it, because email clients are less likely to filter emails from known senders. Your subscribers may also have manually whitelisted your sending address (which you should encourage), and changing the address will mean losing any whitelisting benefit.

Legal Compliance

Most of this book is about guidelines, suggestions, and general tips, but depending on where you and your clients live there may be also legal requirements for any commercial email you send.

The most famous of these laws is of course the dubiously effective *CAN-SPAM Act (2003)*, which applies to US senders of "email whose primary purpose is advertising or promoting a commercial product or service, including content on a website." Processing emails (such as order confirmations and the like) are mostly exempt.

The CAN-SPAM law requires that your emails must:

- have accurate "From" and "To" addresses, email headers, and routing information that identifies the sender
- avoid deceptive or misleading subject lines
- contain an unsubscribe or opt-out mechanism
- identify itself as a commercial email and contain a valid physical address for the sender

The main impact of this law for designers is the need to include the physical address in the design, typically in the footer as you'll have seen. Find out more about CAN-SPAM at the FTC website.[4]

Outside of the USA, there are plenty of similar pieces of legislation, so make certain you know what applies to the emails you're sending. For a head start on finding out laws relevant in your area, visit Mark Brownlow's helpful list.[5]

Unsubscribe Link

Even if there's no legal requirement to have a method of unsubscribing, it's usually a good idea. Giving subscribers a clear and simple way to say "I would like to stop

---

[4] http://www.ftc.gov/bcp/edu/pubs/business/ecommerce/bus61.shtm
[5] http://www.email-marketing-reports.com/canspam/

receiving your emails now" is the best option for all sides. It helps you as the sender, because you avoid the cost of sending an email to a recipient who is only going to trash it anyway. And it leaves your subscriber with a positive experience of your company or service—you give them control in the relationship.

When I review email campaigns, I can sense right in the pixels the grudging way in which some designers give in to the unsubscribe requirement. They hide it in a four-pixel light gray font in the middle of an otherwise unrelated paragraph. It's like playing a particularly frustrating version of "Where's Waldo," and if you don't find him this time he'll knock on your door next week and make you play again.

There's really no point to this. If a person doesn't want to receive your email, they will not read it anyway, and by irritating them and making it difficult you're just increasing the risk of them reporting it as spam. So make your unsubscribe method loud and proud. You can have a bit of fun with it, though.

One Campaign Monitor customer ended their email with "Every person who unsubscribes makes us cry a tear, but if you must: click here." Another email for a nightclub showed some honesty: "If you signed up while drunk you can unsubscribe here."

A person who knows it's super easy to unsubscribe is far more likely to resubscribe later on if they need your information or services again.

Now that we've familiarized ourselves with the design constraints that apply to HTML email, and a few key components we'll be sure to remember, we're ready to begin the actual job of designing the email. But where to start? Fortunately, almost all email designs can be based on an existing website design.

Adapting a Website Design into an Email Design

The typical email design project will be associated with an existing brand, and you'll almost always have a website design in place from which to work. Making your email design feel like it's from the same company—or website—is extremely important. A 2006 survey from Return Path showed that the biggest influence on whether emails were opened was "knowing and trusting the sender."[6] If the email uses recognizable colors, titles, and imagery, the subject line and preview pane will

---

[6] http://returnpath.net/

remind the recipients about the sender of the email, providing the confidence to act.

An email that's visually disconnected from the site it links to will jar, even if it does convince some recipients to click a link.

Don't go crazy and try to replicate the entire website in an email, though. Your design should take the essential feel of the brand (excuse the marketing terms) and translate it into what will work for an email.

Campaign Monitor's own email newsletter template is one example. Compare the current Campaign Monitor home page to the newsletter, both which can be seen in Figure 3.7.

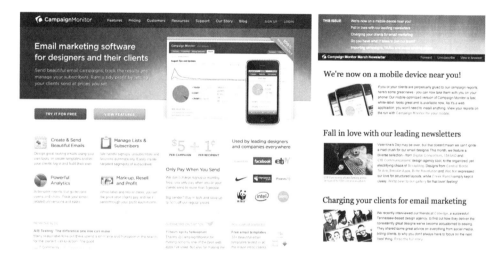

Figure 3.7. Campaign Monitor website and newsletter

Structurally the email is much simpler, consisting of a single column. The email header ties in to the sunburst effect from the website header, but the content has been reordered. At a glance the two images look strongly related, but not identical. This is the level of similarity to aim for: an email that feels as though it's a natural extension of the website. It should stand on its own as a well-designed and readable document, but clearly be part of a bigger design.[7]

---

[7] You can find out more about how the Campaign Monitor newsletter was planned and built at http://www.campaignmonitor.com/blog/post/2677/redesigning-the-campaign-monitor-newsletter/.

Figure 3.8, Figure 3.9, and Figure 3.10 are the current home pages of some other popular services (on the left), and their newsletters (on the right).

Figure 3.8. 37signals home page and newsletter

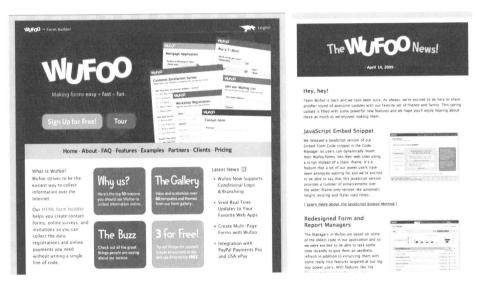

Figure 3.9. Wufoo home page and newsletter

Figure 3.10. Authentic Jobs home page and newsletter

If you see an example of a great newsletter, make sure you click through to the home page of the company or sender and compare them. You'll learn exactly what the designer thought were the key elements of the website design and brand by what they chose to include, and what was left out.

Layout Possibilities

Even in 600 pixels, there are plenty of ways to lay out content. How do designers usually approach an email layout? Figure 3.11 shows some the most popular block-level email layouts, as taken from a typical day of email campaigns sent through Campaign Monitor.

(In truth, these are the most popular layouts once we've excluded the common but horrifying "jumbled mess of unstructured text and images," which remains an unfortunate favorite with many senders.)

Two-column layouts (with about an 80/20 split) are by far the most popular layouts, which was true for websites ten years ago as well. The idea of interspersing two-column blocks with full-width blocks is very popular, and gives the email a more dynamic feel if it's done right. It's also very flexible, and allows you to use a variety of different content types.

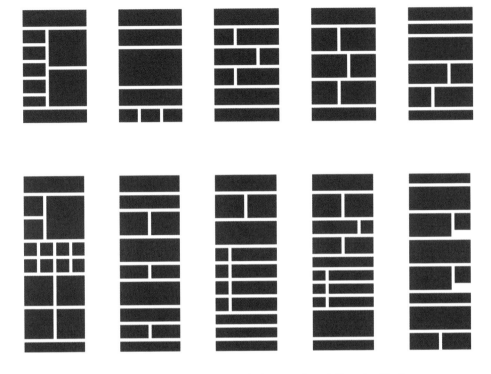

Figure 3.11. The most popular layout variations sent through Campaign Monitor

It's very rare to see more than three columns, and that's hardly surprising given the design constraints I talked about in the section called "The Design Environment for Email". For our example client, you'll remember we came up with this core content list:

- Information on the featured product of the day
- Featured article (building our reputation for knowledge)
- Link to send the email onto a henchmate
- Henching tip of the week

The primary content, then, will be a couple of articles and probably a featured photo. This could easily be achieved in several different layouts, so we have some design flexibility here. If our articles are more than a paragraph or two, it makes sense to give them the biggest chunk of screen space.

For the first issue, we've opted for the layout depicted in Figure 3.12.

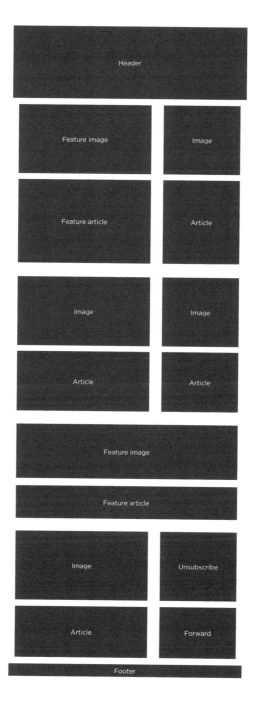

Figure 3.12. A wireframe of the layout for the *Modern Henchman* newsletter

I chose this layout as it gives the main content visual weight and room to be easily understood, but also has a few obvious spots where we can fit in our other promotions. As a basic template, this will work from month to month without requiring a complete redesign. Broad consistency is helpful for your readers to recognize the email and grow used to reading it. It also saves time and lets the content creators focus on the actual writing and editing, rather than reworking the layout with each issue.

If you have a client that sends several different types of content, you can of course create many design variations to suit; you'd still want to make them recognizable as being from the same sender and on the same topic, though.

Remember that the actual content could be shorter than what we were planning on, or longer, or more varied month by month. So our design needs to be flexible enough to hold together over time. Pixel-perfect design never worked very well on the Web, and it certainly won't work in an email client.

Some designers like to create a more detailed mockup at this point, slotting content sections in wherever they fit. You might find the mockup a useful document to show your client before you commit to particular color schemes or layout sizes.

Designing to Meet Business Goals

We can adapt the tone and look of our email from existing materials, if any, and come up with a practical layout for the content. What we need to do now is work out how to put it all together in the most effective way. But what does it mean to have an effective email?

Refer back to Chapter 2, where we completed a client brief for *Modern Henchman* magazine. The brief laid out what our client was expecting to achieve from their email newsletter investment. Taking that brief, we suggested a primary goal: generate at least $400 in sales directly from newsletter subscribers in the first week after each email is sent.

How can the design of the email help meet that goal? Here's the five-second test to see if an email has a clear goal. Glance at the email for just a moment, and answer this question: "What does the designer of this email want me to do first?"

You might answer "read this article" or "look at these photos." More often, though, you'd wind up saying "I have no idea." Let's start with a fairly obvious example, shown in Figure 3.13.

moving to the country!

Great news, we are now settling into our fantastic new offices on the Kingston Estate in Staverton.

It's business as usual for the pulse8 team, just a little more rustic.

Check out our new studio location

Figure 3.13. An email with a clear goal

There's no guessing required here; the person who sent you this email wants you to check out their new studio location. This might seem obvious, but so many emails obscure their main goal with huge headers, waffly introductions, and dozens of links to less important pages.

Another example, from the always-discerning 37signals, is shown in Figure 3.14.

Figure 3.14. 37signals Haystack announcement

This email is clearly intended to introduce Haystack (since renamed Sortfolio), yet there's no need to read the whole email to find out what Haystack is about. Even if you just glance at the email for a few seconds, it has already accomplished its primary goal: you've been made aware of the new service, and you know what it's all about. That's good design!

So, back to *Modern Henchman*. They want to sell $400 of product as a direct result of their email. What does that goal look like in an email? We're going to have to make sure the email lets people know what they can buy, and gives them reasons to actually do this. Here are some ideas of how we can go about accomplishing these goals:

- Use a promo photo of the products we'd most like to sell.
- Use direct language; for example: "Purchase the hat-brim blade today."
- Avoid confusing the message by having too many other links.

A quick glance at the email should have people saying to themselves, "That looks cool, I wonder what it is?"

In addition to the content, our goal could be addressed right in the subject line. Compare these two options:

- *Modern Henchman* newsletter, May 2010 edition
- Weapons on sale: *Modern Henchman* magazine

The second subject line is far more precise, and the reader knows exactly what to expect when they open the email.

Fortunately, no guessing is required as to which one would perform better. As we discussed in Chapter 2, emails are highly measurable. A simple **A/B test** (where part of the subscriber list receives option one; the rest, option two) would quickly show which variant resulted in more opens, clicks, or even purchases.

Before testing, we'll rely on the briefing and goals to decide which options are most likely to be effective. Once the email has been sent, the test results will help to refine the design for the next campaign.

The *Modern Henchman* Newsletter Design

Finally, it's time for the design work. For some people, this is the point to fire up their copy of Photoshop or Fireworks. Others prefer to start with pen and paper, a whiteboard, or charcoal and a convenient cave wall. Whatever works for you is fine.

For the *Modern Henchman* magazine newsletter, we have taken the layout we put together above and inserted some photography from the website. We've also chosen fonts and colors that match those on the website. We had the writers from the website provide us with the content that will be going into the first issue, so we have some subject matter to design around.

The resulting mockup is shown in Figure 3.15.

Figure 3.15. The *Modern Henchman* newsletter mockup

Of course, that's just one example of an HTML email. And while it accomplishes the client's goals admirably, it might not be the sort of design best suited to your particular project. So, to help get your creative juices flowing, the next section is a gallery of some of my favorite HTML email newsletters from which you can draw inspiration.

Gallery of HTML Emails

Scan through these screenshots of some top-notch HTML emails, and think about what they're trying to achieve. They're categorized for convenience, but many of them would fit into multiple categories.

Clear Call to Action

These emails are very clear about what they want the reader to do. Giving your reader one obvious option will significantly increase your clickthrough rate.

The bgroup[8] creative agency's newsletter, shown in Figure 3.16, draws attention to an already giant button with a comical character.

A Monster of an idea for Enterprise Week

To celebrate Enterprise Week, bgroup has created an entrepreneurial poster identifying common breeds of monsterpreneurs. Order your free poster here and see if it features anyone you know.

If you've got an entrepreneurial streak, test it out with our Monsterpreneur Game and see how your friends' scores compare to yours.

Visit thebgroup.co.uk for details of all our most recent news, events and creative work.

The Massodermis
There's no pumice stone large enough to scrape the hardened edges off this fiend. He's seen it all before and he didn't break a sweat the first time.

Problems with this email? View it in your browser.
If you no longer wish to receive bgroup emails, unsubscribe here.

Figure 3.16. bgroup creative newsletter

[8] www.thebgroup.co.uk

The Scrapblog[9] sales email in Figure 3.17 has a call to action that isn't a button, but is nonetheless very compelling, drawing the reader in to learn why they should be ordering before this date.

Figure 3.17. Scrapblog sales email

[9] http://www.scrapblog.com/

The email from Xero,[10] shown in Figure 3.18, uses a more conventional call-to-action button. It's highly effective because of the strong color contrast with the otherwise monochrome theme of the rest of the email.

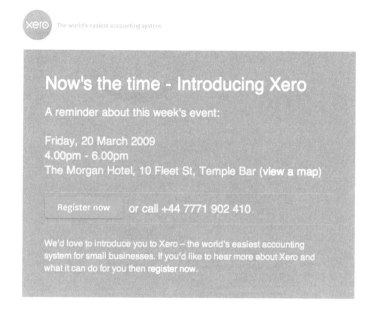

Figure 3.18. Xero event reminder

---

[10] http://www.xero.com/

Structure and Layout

Here are some designs that show how flexible even an environment as limited as email can be.

The email shown in Figure 3.19 for a Belgian design conference[11] makes excellent use of typography and layout to clearly separate its various sections.

Figure 3.19. Week van het ontwerpen conference announcement

[11] http://www.weekvanhetontwerpen.be/

The email from Dekalb Tire, shown in Figure 3.20, also makes excellent use of layout.[12] It uses a few different line thicknesses and textures to delimit sections without making the email appear cluttered.

Figure 3.20. Dekalb Tire sales email

---

[12] http://www.mydekalbtire.com/

Unlike the previous two examples, Figure 3.21 shows an email that uses text as its primary design element, but still manages to create a clear structure through clever use of a three-column layout.

Figure 3.21. Kunstenfestivaldesarts festival announcement

Typography

Although fonts based on Flash and JavaScript are unavailable in email clients, and as we've mentioned it's best not to rely on images for your content, it's still possible to produce beautiful typography in an email.

For a fantastic example, take a look at Figure 3.22, from cabedge.com.[13] Using just a few fonts in varied sizes and colors, combined with a clever idea, the email really catches your interest and relays its message.

Figure 3.22. New phone number announcement from cabedge.com

---

[13] http://cabedge.com/

Figure 3.23 illustrates another great typography-centric email design. Frost Design[14] use a single-column layout very effectively thanks to strong separations.

Figure 3.23. Frost Design newsletter

[14] http://www.frostdesign.com.au/

Even though the email in Figure 3.24 consists mostly of a large image file, it makes the image subservient to the primary content. We talked about using typographic characters as design elements in plain text emails, but Reconsider Design[15] provide an excellent example of how this technique can be applied equally well to HTML emails: the two slash characters (//) that precede each heading provide a strong visual cue, tying the design together. Even better, they work independently of images being enabled.

Figure 3.24. Reconsider newsletter

---

[15] http://www.reconsiderdesign.co.uk/

Special Purpose

Although most of this book is focused around regular email newsletters, there are plenty of other uses for HTML email. Have a look at these standout examples. Unlike newsletters, these special-purpose emails have even greater freedom to center on a single key message or idea.

Figure 3.25 shows a great example of an invitation email. All the key information is presented in a single column, with an interesting theme tying the design together.

Figure 3.25. Invitation: Dr. Flahoo's Halloween Hang Out

Figure 3.26 shows a holiday greeting card sent by cabedge.com. Notice how the graphic at the top reinforces the holiday theme while also serving as a subtle arrow that draws the eye down the the message, which is short and sweet.

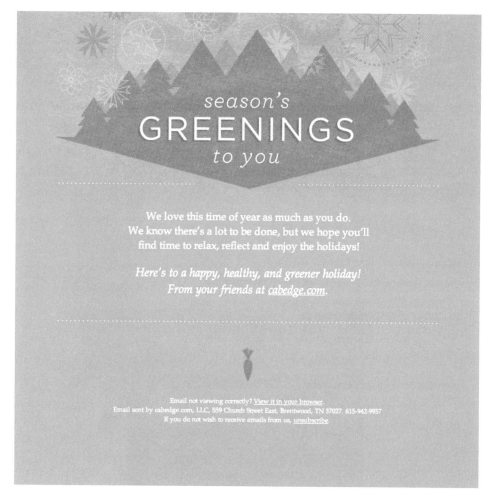

Figure 3.26. Holiday card from cabedge.com

The reminder email from DHL Express[16] shown in Figure 3.27 has a lot of positive features: it uses an image as a supporting element rather than for core content; it has a clearly stated, personal message; and it has an obvious call to action.

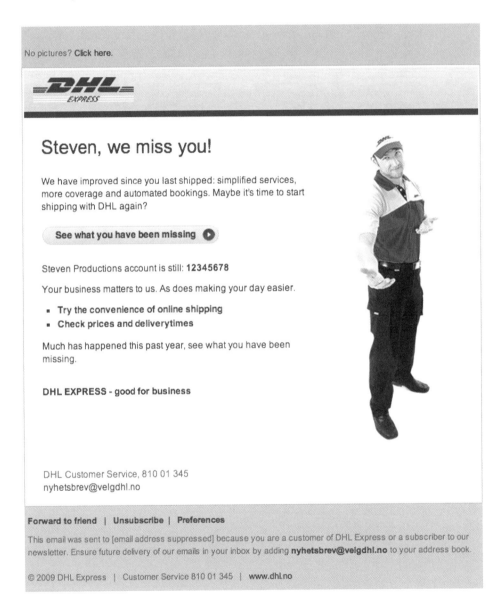

Figure 3.27. Reminder email from DHL Express

Almost Image Free

Just because you use HTML doesn't mean you have to use lots of images. These emails employ striking design without relying on images being downloaded.

This example in Figure 3.28, an invitation to attend an organizational meeting by the Greater Houston Partnership,[17] consists almost exclusively of blocks of text. Yet it uses the features of HTML to make that text clear and readable, conveying its message as simply and directly as possible.

Figure 3.28. GHP invitation email

---

[17] http://www.houston.org/

The product announcement email from Huge Paper[18] in Figure 3.29 makes excellent use of a simple color scheme. By combining this with a clear layout and plenty of whitespace, it's a strong design without relying on images.

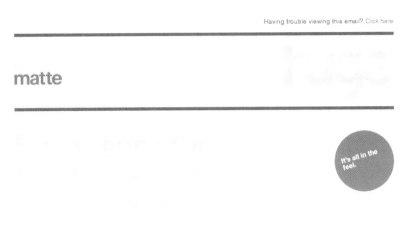

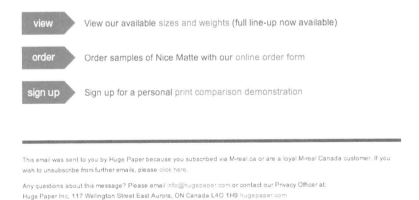

Figure 3.29. Nice Matte announcement from huge

---

[18] http://www.hugepaper.com/

We've already seen part of the pulse8[19] email presented in Figure 3.30 in the section called "Designing to Meet Business Goals", so of course it has a strong call to action. What's even more impressive is that it relies on no images at all, and still conveys its message powerfully.

moving to the country!

Great news, we are now settling into our fantastic new offices on the Kingston Estate in Staverton.

It's business as usual for the pulse8 team, just a little more rustic.

> ## *Check out our new studio location*

Our new address isn't too far from Totnes:
Unit 8/9, Kingston West Drive, Staverton, Totnes, Devon TQ9 6AR

We will shortly be organising an open studio day. In the mean time, feel free to
drop in and check out our new home, we'd love to see you.

ask@pulse8.co.uk | tel: 01803 864545

You have been sent this email because the email address [email address suppressed] has previously opted in
to receive our updates. You can unsubscribe if you wish be removed from the database. Thanks, pulse8.

Registered Company Number: 06987204

Figure 3.30. Moving announcement from pulse8

---

[19] http://www.pulse8.co.uk/

More Places for Email Design Inspiration

Sign up for as many newsletters as you can (use a folder or special email address so that you can easily separate them from your regular email). Reading the actual emails in your own inbox is a different experience than seeing a screenshot in a gallery, so I highly recommend it as a way to immerse yourself in the design language of HTML email.

Even so, there are a few great collections of email designs that are well worth browsing. As you browse, try to work out what the design was intended to achieve.

- Campaign Monitor free templates[20]
- Themeforest templates[21]
- MailChimp free templates[22]
- Campaign Monitor gallery of great designs[23]
- SpamMeltdown email gallery[24]
- Beautiful Email Newsletters Gallery[25]
- Inspirational Newsletter Designs: Flickr Set[26]

Beyond the design galleries, the Web is full of smart discussion about what makes emails actually work. Start here to learn more:

- BeRelevant! Blog[27]
- Email Marketing Voodoo[28]
- The Retail Email Blog[29]

---

[20] http://www.campaignmonitor.com/templates
[21] http://themeforest.net/category/email-templates
[22] http://www.mailchimp.com/resources/html_email_templates/
[23] http://www.campaignmonitor.com/gallery
[24] http://spammeltdown.com/
[25] http://www.beautiful-email-newsletters.com/
[26] http://www.flickr.com/photos/dmadray/sets/72157617876767799/
[27] http://www.b2bemailmarketing.com/
[28] http://emailmarketingvoodoo.com/
[29] http://www.retailemailblog.com/

Conclusion

How did that go? Gather some great ideas? In the next chapter, we'll be taking our designs and turning them into functional HTML emails. There are plenty of tips and tricks, but we'll also be relying heavily on your existing HTML skills.

Be forewarned that you may need to use techniques you thought you'd left behind in the last millennium.

Coding Your Emails

With a well-thought-out content and design plan in place, it's time to dirty our hands with HTML and CSS. By the end of this chapter we'll have produced a solid email template that works in all the major email clients.

What's so hard about HTML emails?

You've built a ton of websites, you can write HTML and CSS in your sleep, and you have a big poster on your wall of Jeffrey Zeldman.[1] So how hard can it be to build an HTML email? Well, it's harder than you might think.

In the broader web design world, we've been through the browser wars where Netscape and Internet Explorer fought each other to introduce competing ways to code just about everything. Thanks to the Web Standards Project and associated efforts, modern web browsers are much more consistent than they were ten years ago.

---

[1] For the uninitiated, Jeffrey Zeldman is one of the co-founders of the Web Standards Project, and also of the influential online publication *A List Apart [http://alistapart.com]*.

Unfortunately, while that war was being fought, email clients like Outlook and Lotus Notes were apparently off hiding in the marketing department behind a very expensive beanbag chair, and were left behind.

Even worse than not trying to improve their HTML and CSS rendering, some email clients have actually gone backwards. Three years ago, Microsoft decided Outlook 2007 would stop using Internet Explorer to render HTML emails. Before you get all excited, they were replacing it with Microsoft Word. Yes, that Microsoft Word, the word processor. In one version, Outlook went from being decent and understandable to downright terrible at displaying HTML emails from anyone except other Outlook users.

Outlook 2007 is a hugely popular email client, but that's not the only problem: building HTML for email means you're dealing with more than four or five major web browsers, and 12 to 15 different email clients, each with solid market share.

Some of them are great, like Apple Mail. A design that works in Safari will be perfect in Apple Mail. Some, like Outlook, are horrible and will cause dizziness, hair loss, and heart palpitations. In between are a whole slew of different rendering constraints, quirks, and inconsistencies.

So there's a challenge for web designers. How do you take your 2010 web design skills and apply them to email clients with last millennium's capabilities? Don't despair, because it's possible to succeed with a little bit of knowledge and willingness to test. You might even save your hairline.

Guidelines for a Solid HTML Email Template

If you've been building websites for long enough to remember the glory days of GeoCities and Angelfire, you probably built your first websites using tables for layout. Building an HTML email today will take you back to those heady times, although with rather less use of the <hr> tag.

Go ahead and stick a bookmark in this section, because you'll want to come back to it every time you start building a new email template. I'll cover the tips and tricks that make it possible to attain good results for as many of your—or your clients'—readers as possible.

Know Your Audience

The first step in building a successful HTML email is to know how it will be read. If the subscribers are all going to be reading your email on their company-provided BlackBerry devices, you might decide to use plain text, for example. In most cases there'll be a mix of email clients in use, but there are a few ways to find out. Campaign Monitor publishes some overall statistics for email client usage[2] that give a broad overview, albeit with some limitations.

There's no guarantee that these reflect your audience, though. A tool like Fingerprint[3] can give you a better idea of what your readers are actually using. Some email service providers will give you a report for each campaign, listing the email client for each subscriber where available.

What you're looking for in these reports is your lowest common denominator. If there's 30% using Lotus Notes 7, for example, you'll need to make sure you specifically test in that client before sending. A particular version of an email client might be relevant—Outlook 2003 will cause you far fewer headaches than Outlook 2007, and in some cases your list might only use one version.

If you've never sent to this list before, you might just have to test in every client you can find, and make some educated guesses about the kind of audience with which you're dealing. Are they likely to be using mobile phones to read email, or locked-down corporate servers?

Maybe they're all individuals using Hotmail and Yahoo addresses, which are at least easy to test in. Whatever you know about your audience, make yourself some notes about what email clients you most want to check every time you send.

Tables: Not Just for Data

The single most important guideline for HTML emails is that CSS layout just doesn't work. The major email clients either offer no support at all, or mangle it in myriad frustratingly different ways.

---

[2] http://www.campaignmonitor.com/stats/email-clients/

[3] http://fingerprintapp.com/

Using CSS instead of tables was the battle cry of the web standards war, but coding HTML emails means raising the white flag and giving in. Unless you're building an *extremely* simple email, or your whole audience is using a more modern email reading tool, it's back to those all encompassing <table> tags.

Gmail, Outlook 2007, Lotus Notes, and no doubt many more all have big issues with floated elements, and are even wildly unreliable with margins and padding. You'll want to set up some structural HTML tables to make sure you end up with an email that at least holds together well.

There are some problems using tables, too, as learned the hard way by many designers. Here are a few tips for dealing with them:

Set Widths in Each Cell Rather than on the Table

The combination of widths on the table, widths on the cells, HTML margins and padding, and CSS margins and padding can be chaotic. Simplify your code, and your life, by setting only on each cell:

```
<table cellspacing="0" cellpadding="0" border="0">
  <tr>
    <td width="150"></td>
    <td width="350"></td>
  </tr>
</table>
```

Email clients are unreliable when it comes to deducing the correct width of a cell, so it's safest to explicitly set one. Pixel widths are the most reliable, as using percentages can give you some wacky results, especially when using nested tables.

To set your cell padding, either set it once on the whole table with the cellpadding parameter, or use CSS to set padding in individual cells. Mixing the two is likely to cause problems, and is best avoided.

Nest Tables for Consistent Spacing

Even when margins and padding are supported by most email clients, results will be inconsistent. If the spacing is critical to you, try nesting tables inside your main table instead. Old school!

Set a Background Color on a Container Table

Some email clients will ignore a background on the <body> tag, or one that's set in your style sheet. Having a wrapping table around all your content and setting a bgcolor attribute on it will work around this issue.

Whitespace Does Matter

Theoretically, whitespace in HTML files should be ignored, but in practice it can cause all sorts of rendering quirks—especially if you have whitespace between table cells. Make a habit of removing any spaces between the closing tag of one cell and the opening tag of the next to avoid unsightly gaps and layout problems.

Use Inline CSS

This is where the C for Cascading in CSS comes in handy. Applying a style inline gives it priority over styles further away (such as webmail client styles), and also works around the email clients that strip out CSS from the head or external CSS files.

Here's a quick refresher in case you've not used inline CSS for a while (or ever, if you started web design after 2000).

A style applied to p elements in a separate style sheet or in the head of your HTML page might look like this:

```
p {
  line-height: 1.5em;
  margin: 0px 0px 10px 0px;
}
```

These styles will apply to all paragraphs in your page, but if the style is stripped out (as Gmail will do), the paragraphs will be styled according to whatever default the email client uses, or the webmail client's own style sheet.

Applying the style inline means styling each individual p element throughout your content:

```
<p style="line-height:1.5em;margin:0px 0px 10px 0px;">Lorem … </p>
```

You'll achieve more consistent results if you apply styles in this way for all the relevant elements in your HTML email.

When you start doing this, you'll quickly realize that it's tiresome work repeating the same styles over and over in your HTML (a lot like `<font>` tags used to be). Lucky for us, there are a few ways to save time:

- Don't inline your styles until you've finished the coding—develop it all using a `<style>` tag in your `head`, and only once you've made all the changes do you apply them inline. This saves having to go back and edit 20 instances of the same style.

- Use an email service or tool that will automatically inline your CSS for you. Campaign Monitor, for example, will optionally take styles from the `head` or from an external file and automatically apply each style to the appropriate elements inline when you import your campaign.

There are several tools that will take an HTML page and style sheet, and then spit out your page with the CSS all inlined. My favorite is Premailer,[4] which will also give you useful advice about unsupported CSS.

There are certain styles that perform poorly inline—you're unable to specify `:hover` states for links, for example. It's generally worth keeping the styles in the `head` as well as inline—the extra download size is outweighed by the benefit of covering all your bases.

Avoid Relying on Images

We already touched on this in the section called "Image Blocking" in Chapter 3, but it's worth revisiting.

Do you remember the web designer term "slicing"? When websites used to be constructed by designing a page-sized image and cutting it into little sections, which were then reassembled into tables and stuck on a page?

That used to be a very common technique for working around browser inconsistencies. Sadly, the same technique lives on in many email designers' toolboxes, and

---

[4] http://premailer.dialect.ca/

even the biggest companies send out HTML emails that are nothing more than a collection of images.

While it certainly reduces the time spent developing the email, the benefits end there. Unlike web browsers, email clients routinely block images from downloading until the reader clicks a special button or link, as shown in Figure 4.1.

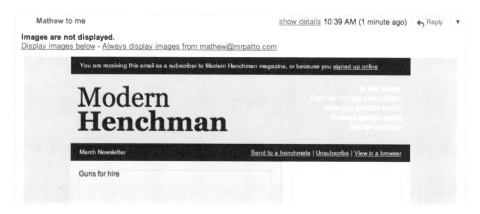

Figure 4.1. Image of a "display images in this email" link

Research over the last few years has shown that a significant percentage (some estimate up to 40%) of email recipients never enable images at all. Add to that all the people who fail to realize they *could* show images, and you have a huge chunk of recipients who will not see your logo, product photo, or animated mailbox.

The default image blocking settings for various email clients are shown in Table 4.1 (you can find an up-to-date version of this table online).[5] I'll be explaining what the last column (trusted sender) means very shortly. For now, just pay attention to the second column: it shows whether images are displayed or not by default in each of the clients.

---

[5] http://www.campaignmonitor.com/image-blocking

Table 4.1. Image Blocking in Email Clients

Client	Default img display	Trusted sender img display
Yahoo Mail	✓	✗
Yahoo Mail Beta	✓	✓
Windows Live Mail	✗	✓
Gmail	✗	✓
.Mac	✓	✗
Hotmail	✓	✓
AOL Web	✓	✓
Apple Mail	✓	✗
Thunderbird	✓	✓
Outlook 2007	✗	✓
Outlook 2003	✗	✓
Outlook Express	✓	✗
Lotus Notes	✓	✓
Eudora	✓	✗
Entourage	✓	✗
AOL Desktop	✗	✓

Unless you know for sure that your audience is only reading email in Apple Mail, for example, you need to assume that a decent number of people will not see your images (since a number of popular clients, including Gmail, Windows Live, and Outlook 2003 and 2007 block images by default). So that beautiful sales newsletter, which is supposed to appear as seen in Figure 4.2, will actually look as shown in Figure 4.3.

Figure 4.2. An all-image newsletter

Figure 4.3. The same newsletter, with images turned off

You can imagine the impact that will have on the success of your campaign! So what's the alternative? There are actually a few ways to work around image blocking.

Become a Known Sender

Most email clients allow recipients to automatically display images when a message is from a known sender (senders appearing in whitelists, contact lists, or address books). The final column in Table 4.1 shows which clients will allow recipients to override their image blocking setting for trusted senders.

You'll want to encourage your subscribers to add the "From" address you use to their whitelist. You can have a note right on your sign-up form that asks them to do this, so that the first email they receive will display images. And if you choose to send one, you can also include a more in-depth note in the confirmation email that's sent when people join your list.

In your actual email campaigns you can do the same. To be more helpful, put a page on your site with instructions for how to add an address to the whitelist for different email clients, and link to it.[6]

Living without Images

There will always be people who by choice or chance never enable images for your campaigns, so the design needs to take that into account. Follow a few simple guidelines to improve your results:

Don't use an image as the first item in your email

Remember that many email programs will use a small preview window, and if the only element that fits there is an undisplayed image, the email might as well be blank. Start with some useful HTML text content that lets your readers know what they're going to receive. It might give them a reason to bother downloading the images.

Use `alt` attributes

Just like you do for a website, make sure to have useful `alt` attributes for each image. In some cases, they will show up when the image is blocked, and can provide a good backup. Unfortunately they won't always be displayed, or be displayed in full. Check Table 4.2 to see how common email clients will handle `alt` attributes.

---

[6] A good resource for whitelisting instructions is http://www.emaildeliveryjedi.com/mywhitelist.htm.

Table 4.2. `alt` Attribute Support

Client	Renders `alt`	Comments
Yahoo Mail	✗	N/A
Yahoo Mail Beta	✓	Applies CSS font-styling to `alt` attributes.
Windows Live Mail	✗	N/A
Gmail	Sometimes	Contingent on text length
.Mac	Sometimes	Contingent on text length
Hotmail	✗	N/A
Apple Mail	✗	Replaces `alt` text with question mark icon.
Thunderbird	✓	Applies CSS font-styling to `alt` text.
Outlook 2007	Sort of	Replaces `alt` text with security message.
Outlook 2003	✓	Applies CSS font styling to `alt` text.
Outlook Express	✓	Applies CSS font styling to `alt` text.
Eudora	Sort of	Replaces `alt` text with URL to image.

Use captions for important images

If you have an image that contains important content (as opposed to being a decorative element), use a text caption to describe it. That way, even if the image is not displayed readers will have access to the email's full content. This is more reliable than `alt` attributes; as we've seen, `alt` attribute rendering is highly variable between email clients.

Always have text and images

If you have a balance of HTML text and some images, then the email is useful even without images. If the email entirely consists of images that are blocked, the email is a waste of time.

Consider whether you need images at all

Sometimes imagery is essential. For a great example, see the FontShop newsletter, which displays samples of new fonts.[7] Without the images, it's a lot less

---

[7] http://www.fontshop.com/

useful, so they're definitely worth including. The FontShop audience is also more likely to be displaying images at all times.

For some cases, though, imagery is unnecessary. Consider a transactional email like an order confirmation. It needs to be clear and able to be scanned, but images aren't going to contain vital content. So you may choose to spend your time on typography, formatting, and fine-tuning the content.

Use a recognizable logo for those who'll be able to see it, but avoid relying on the images to make your point for you. Ensure that part of your campaign sending process is viewing the email without any images loaded, the way a lot of your recipients will be seeing it.

Dissuade clients who want all-image emails

Web designers often tell me that they personally know better than to send purely image emails, but their clients want everything to look perfect. Here's the point—it's our job as designers to show our clients why that is such a bad idea. Sit them down and show them what their email will look like without images. Ask them, "Would you click through on this blank page?"

Remind them that perhaps 30% of people will be seeing exactly that, which could equate to hundreds or thousands of people who might hit Delete and never bother loading those images. This is a case where we need to give clients what they actually need, rather than what they think they want.

 ## Another Reason to Avoid All-image Emails

Spam filters often use the ratio of images versus text as a flag to gauge whether an email is legitimate. All-image emails are more likely to be marked as spam than mixed content emails.

Other Guidelines

These are the most important guidelines for a reliable HTML email template, but there are other relevant odds and ends that are necessary to keep in mind:

Store the email images on a web server—preferably in a folder that's separate from your website's images (for example, in a folder called **/images/email**), and don't delete them. Some people open emails weeks or months later, the same way people use bookmarks to return to websites.

Use the `target="_blank"` attribute for your `<a>` tags, so that people who read with webmail services don't have the requested page appear within their webmail interface.

CSS Support in Email Clients

There are some designers who will tell you that you have to use `<font>` tags because CSS never works in email clients. That's just not the case, and there's a significant body of tests that confirm it.

You can safely leave the `<font>` tags in the bottom drawer with your Pogs and Tamagotchis, but there are a lot of cases where you can't use modern CSS techniques. Table 4.4 through to Table 4.10 on the following pages show which of the most common CSS selectors and properties are supported, and which are not, across popular desktop, mobile, and web email clients.

You'll notice that support for many properties you take for granted when developing web pages is inconsistent. Lest you think you can safely write off any of these clients, Table 4.3 shows their current estimated market shares.

Table 4.3. Market Share by Client

Outlook 2003	Yahoo Mail	Yahoo Classic	Live Hotmail	Apple Mail	Outlook 2007	Gmail	Apple iPhone	Lotus Notes 6/7	Lotus Notes 8.5	AOL Desk 10
32%	15%		15%	6%	5%	5%	5%	2%		2%

The latest and most complete versions of these tables are available online.[8]

---

[8] http://www.campaignmonitor.com/css

Table 4.4. link and style Elements

	Outlook 2003	Yahoo Mail	Yahoo Classic	Live Hotmail	Apple Mail	Outlook 2007	Gmail	Apple iPhone	Lotus Notes 6/7	Lotus Notes 8.5	AOL Desk 10
style in head	✓	✓	✓	✓	✓	✓	✗	✓	✗	✓	✓
style in body	✓	✓	✓	✓	✓	✓	✗	✓	✗	✓	✓
link in head	✓	✓	✓	✓	✓	✓	✗	✓	✓	✓	✓
link in body	✓	✓	✓	✓	✓	✓	✗	✓	✗	✓	✓

Table 4.5. Selectors

Selector	Outlook 2003	Yahoo Mail	Yahoo Classic	Live Hotmail	Apple Mail	Outlook 2007	Gmail	Apple iPhone	Lotus Notes 6/7	Lotus Notes 8.5	AOL Desk 10
e	✓	✓	✓	✓	✓	✓	✗	✓	✗	✓	✓
*	✓	✓	✗	✓	✓	✗	✗	✓	✗	✓	✓
e.class	✓	✓	✓	✓	✓	✓	✗	✓	✗	✓	✓
#id	✓	✓	✓	✗	✓	✓	✗	✓	✗	✓	✓
e:link	✓	✓	✓	✓	✓	✓	✗	✓	✗	✓	✓
e:active, e:hover	✓	✓	✓	✓	✓	✗	✗		✗	✓	✓
e:first-line	✓	✗	✓	✗	✓	✗	✗	✓	✗	✓	✓
e:first-letter	✓	✗	✓	✗	✓	✗	✗	✓	✗	✓	✓
e > f	✗	✓	✓	✗	✓	✗	✗	✗	✗	✗	✗
e:focus	✗	✓	✓	✗	✓	✗	✗	✓	✗	✗	✗
e + f	✗	✗	✗	✗	✓	✗	✗	✓	✗	✗	✗
e[foo]	✗	✓	✓	✗	✓	✗	✗	✓	✗	✗	✗

Table 4.6. Text and Fonts

Property	Outlook 2003	Yahoo Mail	Yahoo Classic	Live Hotmail	Apple Mail	Outlook 2007	Gmail	Apple iPhone	Lotus Notes 6/7	Lotus Notes 8.5	AOL Desk 10
direction	✓	✓	✓	✓	✓	✗	✗	✓	✗	✓	✓
font	✓	✓	✓	✓	✓	✗	✗	✓	✗	✓	✓
font-family	✓	✓	✓	✓	✓	✓	✓	✓	✓	✓	✓
font-style	✓	✓	✓	✓	✓	✓	✓	✓	✓	✓	✓
font-variant	✓	✓	✓	✓	✓	✓	✓	✓	✗	✓	✓
font-size	✓	✓	✓	✓	✓	✓	✓	✓	✓	✓	✓
font-weight	✓	✓	✓	✓	✓	✓	✓	✓	✓	✓	✓
letter-spacing	✓	✓	✓	✓	✓	✓	✓	✓	✗	✓	✓
line-height	✓	✓	✓	✓	✓	✓	✓	✓	✗	✓	✓
text-align	✓	✓	✓	✓	✓	✓	✓	✓	✓	✓	✓
text-decoration	✓	✓	✓	✓	✓	✓	✓	✓	✓	✓	✓
text-indent	✓	✓	✓	✓	✓	✓	✓	✓	✗	✓	✓
text-transform	✓	✓	✓	✓	✓	✓	✓	✓	✗	✓	✓
white-space	✗	✓	✓	✓	✓	✗	✓	✓	✗	✗	✗
word-spacing	✓	✓	✓	✓	✓	✗	✓	✓	✗	✓	✓
vertical-align	✓	✓	✓	✓	✓	✗	✓	✓	✗	✓	✓

Table 4.7. Color and Background

Property	Outlook 2003	Yahoo Mail	Yahoo Classic	Live Hotmail	Apple Mail	Outlook 2007	Gmail	Apple iPhone	Lotus Notes 6/7	Lotus Notes 8.5	AOL Desk 10
color	✓	✓	✓	✓	✓	✓	✓	✓	✓	✓	✓
background	✓	✓	✓	✗	✓	partial/buggy	partial/buggy	✓	✗	✗	✓
background-color	✓	✓	✓	✓	✓	✓	✓	✓	✗	✓	✓
background-image	✓	✓	✓	✗	✓	✗	✗	✓	✗	✗	✓
background-position	✓	✓	✓	✗	✓	✗	✗	✓	✗	✗	✓
background-repeat	✓	✓	✓	✗	✓	✗	✗	✓	✗	✗	✓

Table 4.8. Box Model

Property	Outlook 2003	Yahoo Mail	Yahoo Classic	Live Hotmail	Apple Mail	Outlook 2007	Gmail	Apple iPhone	Lotus Notes 6/7	Lotus Notes 8.5	AOL Desk 10
border	✓	✓	✓	✓	✓	✓	✓	✓	✗	✓	✓
height	✓	✓	✓	✓	✓	✗	✓	✓	✗	✓	✓
margin	✓	✓	✓	✗	✓	✓	✓	✓	✗	✓	✓
padding	✓	✓	✓	✓	✓	partial/buggy	✓	✓	✗	✓	✓
width	✓	✓	✓	✓	✓	✗	✓	✓	✗	✓	✓

Table 4.9. Positioning and Display

Property	Outlook 2003	Yahoo Mail	Yahoo Classic	Live Hotmail	Apple Mail	Outlook 2007	Gmail	Apple iPhone	Lotus Notes 6/7	Lotus Notes 8.5	AOL Desk 10
bottom	✓	✗	✗	✗	✓	✗	✗	✓	✗	✓	✓
clear	✓	✓	✓	✓	✓	✗	✓	✓	✗	✓	✓
clip	✓	✗	✗	✗	✓	✗	✗	✓	✗	✗	✓
cursor	✓	✓	✓	✓	✓	✗	✗	✗	✗	✓	✓
display	✓	✓	✓	✓	✓	✗	✓	✓	✓	✓	✓
float	✓	✓	✓	✓	✓	✗	✓	✓	✗	✓	✓
left	✓	✗	✗	✗	✓	✗	✗	✓	✗	✓	✓
opacity	✗	✗	✗	✗	✓	✗	✗	✓	✗	✗	✓
overflow	✓	✓	✓	✓	✓	✗	✓	✗	✗	✗	✓
position	✓	✗	✗	✗	✓	✗	✗	✓	✗	✓	✓
right	✓	✗	✗	✗	✓	✗	✗	✓	✗	✓	✓
top	✓	✗	✗	✗	✓	✗	✗	✓	✗	✓	✓
visibility	✓	✓	✓	✓	✓	✗	✓	✓	✗	✗	✓
z-index	✓	✗	✗	✗	✓	✓	✗	✓	✗	✓	✓

Table 4.10. Lists and Tables

Property	Outlook 2003	Yahoo Mail	Yahoo Classic	Live Hotmail	Apple Mail	Outlook 2007	Gmail	Apple iPhone	Lotus Notes 6/7	Lotus Notes 8.5	AOL Desk 10
list-style-image	✓	✓	✓	✗	✓	✗	✗	✓	✗	✗	✓
list-style-position	✓	✓	✓	✓	✓	✗	✓	✓	✗	✗	✓
list-style-type	✓	✓	✓	✓	✓	✗	✓	✓	✓	✓	✓
border-collapse	✓	✓	✗	✓	✓	✓	✓	✓	✓	✓	✓
border-spacing	✗	✓	✓	✗	✓	✗	✓	✓	✗	✗	✗
caption-side	✗	✗	✗	✓	✗	✗	✓	✗	✗	✗	✗
empty-cells	✗	✓	✓	✓	✓	✗	✓	✓	✗	✗	✗
table-layout	✓	✓	✓	✓	✓	✓	✓	✓	✗	✓	✓

You'll want to refer to these tables when building templates, as a quick way of seeing which selectors and properties are safe to work with, and which ones you need to watch. Even trickier, you'll see inconsistent support for some elements, which will work in certain combinations but not in others, so what works in one email might fail in another.

There's no avoiding the testing process, but the CSS support charts will cut out a lot of the frustration for you. Once you've built a few templates, you'll start to know from memory the quickest way to achieve a solid result.

Webmail clients can be a special case when it comes to HTML email rendering. For example, Gmail comes in at least two different versions, and in Campaign Monitor's testing we've seen variations in how the same email appears depending on which version you're working in. It also strips all CSS in your document's head (whether in a style element or a separate style sheet referred to in a link), and is the main reason I recommend applying all your styles inline.

What Other Technologies Can You Use in HTML Email?

The modern Web contains a lot more than HTML, CSS, and images. JavaScript, audio, Flash, video, animations, and forms are all part of a designer's toolkit. Which of these work in email clients? This section outlines the current state of play.

What Technologies *Should* You Use?

Even if you *can* use a certain technique or medium, you might not want to. People go to your website by choice, typically: they go when they want to and with an understanding of what to expect. An email is an entirely different environment from a website (as discussed in the section called "The Design Environment for Email" in Chapter 3), and having sound or video playing inside an email is more likely to irritate than entertain.

For some emails and some subscribers it might be okay, but be very cautious about disrupting your readers' expectations.

Scripting in Emails

The short answer is that scripting is unsupported in emails. This is hardly surprising, given the obvious security risks involved with a script running inside an application that has all that personal information stored in it.

Webmail clients are mostly running the interface in JavaScript and are not keen on your email interfering with that, and desktop client filters often consider JavaScript to be an indicator of spam or phishing emails.

Even in the cases where it might run, there really is little benefit to scripting in emails. Keep your emails as straight HTML and CSS, and avoid the hassle.

Flash

In the web browser market, Adobe Flash is almost ubiquitous (except on iPhones and iPads, of course), but in the email client world Flash is barely existent. In most cases it's completely absent, and even the fallback image you can select won't show up.

The details of the current level of Flash support are shown in Table 4.11.[9]

---

[9] Visit http://www.campaignmonitor.com/resources/entry/673/using-flash-in-email/ for details on how the testing was done.

Table 4.11. Flash Support in Email Clients

Client	Displayed by Default	Alternate Content Displayed	Security Warning
Outlook 2003	✗	✗	✓
Outlook Express	✗	✗	✓
Thunderbird	✗	✗	✗
Eudora 7	✗	✗	✗
AOL 9	✗	✗	✗
Lotus Notes	✗	✗	✗
Apple Mail	✓	Doesn't matter	✗
Eudora	✗	✗	✗
Entourage	✗	✗	✗
Gmail	✗	✗	✗
Hotmail	✗	✗	✗
Yahoo Mail	✗	✗	✗
Windows Live Mail (beta)	✗	✗	✗

Using Flash in your emails should be avoided for the present, as it just doesn't work. Unsurprisingly, this has a considerable influence on the effectiveness of video in email, which is our next topic.

Video

Video can be a very persuasive medium—presenting action rather than just showing a static photo or text description. Whether people actually want to be watching a video in their email rather than on a website is an open question.

As of 2010, there are a lot of different ways that video theoretically could be included in an email message, but in practice most of them won't work for the majority of recipients. Campaign Monitor has tested the following techniques and formats for live video in an email: Flash, QuickTime, Windows Media, animated GIFs (streamed and embedded), Java Applets, embedded MPEGs, and streamed HTML5 video.

The detailed results are shown in Table 4.12.

Table 4.12. Video Support in Email Clients

Client	Flash	QuickTime	Windows Media	Animated GIF	Java Applet	Embedded MPEG	Embedded Animated GIF
AOL Desktop 10.1	✗	✗	✗	✓	✗	✗	✓
Apple Mail	✓	✓	✓	✓	✗	✗	✓
Entourage	✗	✗	✗	✓	✗	✗	✓
Lotus Notes 6.5	✗	✗	✗	✓	✓	✗	✓
Lotus Notes 7	✗	✗	✗	✓	✓	✗	✓
Lotus Notes 8	✗	✗	✗	✓	✗	✗	✓
Outlook 2003	✗	✗	✗	✓	✗	✓	✓
Outlook 2007	✗	✗	✗	✓	✗	✗	✓
Thunderbird	✗	✗	✗	✓	✗	✗	✓
Windows Mail	✗	✗	✗	✓	✗	✗	✓
AOL Web	✗	✗	✗	✓	✗	✗	✓
Gmail	✗	✗	✗	✓	✗	✗	✓
MobileMe	✗	✗	✗	✓	✗	✗	✗
Windows Live Hotmail	✗	✗	✗	✓	✗	✗	✓
Yahoo Mail	✗	✗	✗	✓	✗	✗	✓
BlackBerry Bold	✗	✗	✗	✓	✗	✗	✓
iPhone 2.2	✗	✗	✗	✓	✗	✗	✓
Windows Mobile 5	✗	✗	✗	✗	✗	✗	✗
Windows Mobile 6	✗	✗	✗	✓	✗	✗	✓

As you can see, animated GIFs do have solid support, although they're still subject to image blocking just like static images. In addition, Outlook 2007 will only show the first frame of the animation.

Personally I recommend a still simpler approach: take a screengrab of your video with the player chrome (and ideally a big honking "play" button), and put that into your email. Make it a link to view the video on your website (and link up a caption underneath it too). It's one additional click, but it's guaranteed to work for everyone.

Forms

Having an email contain a live form is a great idea—it's easy for your readers to fill in some details and RSVP, or answer a survey. Unfortunately, the support for forms in email clients is quite inconsistent. Some clients will put up scary-looking security warnings when the reader tries to use a form, and others will just disable the form so it's unable to be sent.

A lot of people might be able to use a form, but the rest will see a form that does nothing at all, which is a fairly bad experience. Again, the recommended approach is to link to a form on your website, where you know it will work.

The level of form support in common clients is shown in Table 4.13.

Table 4.13. Form Support in Email Clients

Client	Form is displayed	Form is functional
.Mac	✓	✗
Yahoo Mail	✓	✓
Yahoo Mail Classic	✓	✗
AOL Webmail	✓	✗
Gmail	✓	✓
Windows Live Hotmail	✓	✗
Apple Mail	✓	✓
Thunderbird	✓	✓
Penelope (Eudora 8)	✓	✓
Outlook 2007	✗	✗
Outlook 2003	✓	✗
Outlook Express	✓	✓
Windows Live Mail	✓	✓
Lotus Notes 8	✓	✓
Entourage	✓	✓

Testing

If you learn just one lesson from this book (I'm aiming for at least three), let it be this: always, always, always test your emails before you send them out.

There is no worse feeling in the world than hitting that Send button, and then spotting a typo in the very first heading. Well, okay, there are some worse feelings than that. Actually, heaps of them. Still, you take my point.

At Campaign Monitor, we once instructed 70,000+ subscribers to "ass your content" instead of "add your content," which generated quite a few replies, as you might imagine. Luckily, most people are understanding, but that's not always the case.

Once an email has been sent out, it's impossible to take it back. A website can be updated in a moment, but emails live out their separate lives in a million different inboxes, beyond reach.

There are quite a few methods and elements to test. Obviously, you'll have all the copy spell-checked, sanity-checked, and rechecked by a person other than you.

When it comes to the design and build, testing can be a bit time-consuming. There are so many different email clients to look at, versions of those clients, and platform differences that it can be overwhelming.

Fortunately, there are a few great services around that take a lot of the pain out of checking your email in multiple email clients:

- Litmus email testing[10]
- Campaign Monitor design and spam testing[11]
- MailChimp's Inbox Inspector[12]

Each service will take your HTML email and give you back a series of screenshots showing how your email renders in a number of different email clients. You can typically scroll through the whole email, see it with images blocked or images loaded, and gain a fairly good idea if there is a problem you need to fix.

Given more time and access to all the many email clients already set up, it would be better to physically interact with each one, but in practice these testing services are a huge time saver and well worth the cost.

In the quite likely case that something is not working right (content being cut off or displayed in the wrong place, or any number of quirky behaviors), the troubleshooting process begins. If you're lucky, the problem client will be one like Gmail or Outlook that's easy to get your hands on.

Then you can tweak and test a few times to make it work again, and perhaps run another full design test to make sure nothing else broke during the fixes.

---

[10] http://litmusapp.com/
[11] http://www.campaignmonitor.com/testing/
[12] http://www.mailchimp.com/features/power_features/inbox_inspector/

Sometimes it will be a more difficult client, such as a particular version of Lotus Notes. These can be tough to troubleshoot, and you might need the help of a reader or colleague who can run some tests for you.

This process can be quite a long one, but once you have a robust template in place it will be reused over and over for future campaigns, and can often be adapted to suit multiple designs. So the time will be well spent.

Building the *Modern Henchman* Newsletter

In the final part of this chapter we'll look at the code required for the *Modern Henchman* newsletter, which has been developed and tested according to the guidelines we've covered.

You can download this template for free with the code archive for this book[13] and use it as a base for your own designs, if you like.

For our client, the *Modern Henchman* magazine, we're trying to create a solid template that will be reused each month without requiring stacks of extra time in design or testing. So we need to develop an email that has a structure that can handle longer or shorter content without breaking apart.

Figure 4.4 shows a reminder of what we want the final product to look like.

---

[13] http://sitepoint.com/books/htmlemail1/code.php

You are receiving this email as a subscriber to Modern Henchman magazine, or because you signed up online

Modern Henchman

In this issue:
Don't let him get away again!
Henchman to supervillain?
Hot Hats for Henchman
Lair maintenance for beginners

<$currentmonthname$> Newsletter   Send to a henchmate | Unsubscribe | View in a browser

Don't let him get away again!

We uncover the 10 most common tricks superspies use to escape even the most fearsome of death traps. You'll never let the boss down again!

Read the Top 10

Henchman to supervillain?

Take your henching career to the next level with our easy step guide to a brand new you.

Can you make it?

Hot Hats for Henchman

Stand out from the crowd with this years selection of henchman headwear that's both attractive and functional. Available in a range of fashion colours, and perfect for the balding baddy.

Beware, not every head can handle a hat, so take our hat quiz before you buy.

Meet the milliner

Never outshoot the boss!

Henchman Ettiquette Expert Aunty Blake answers your tricky questions about showing up the boss in a fire fight.

Read more

Diary of a Henchman

Finally, the explosive anonymous revelations of a henchman who has worked with some of history's greatest villains. You won't believe what goes on when the giant death ray is turned off.

We've got advance copies for every new subscriber to the print version of Modern Henchman, so don't delay subscribe today.

➤ **Send to a henchmate**

Do your henching colleagues need some tips? Why not send this email to them.

Lair maintenance for beginners

The boss has captured his arch enemy for the third time, but the laser mounts keep slipping off the sharks and the aquarium guy can't come until Saturday! Don't panic, just follow our simple illustrated guides and you'll be indispensable.

Read more

🚫 **Is the thrill gone?**

If you're not interested in being the best Henchman you can be, please unsubscribe.

The Modern Henchman logo and design are trademarks of Hench International Pty Ltd

Figure 4.4. Screenshot of the *Modern Henchman* newsletter

Building the Framework

Beginning from the top, we have an introductory section that should show in the preview pane for most readers. It will contain a simplified list of contents for the email and a reminder of why people are receiving the newsletter.

Even with images turned off, that text will be visible, and it's a great opportunity to convince people to read on. We'll also put an unsubscribe link right up top, for those who are no longer interested. As we've discussed, it's much better to let them unsubscribe easily than to force them to mark it as spam.

Below the introduction is the masthead, which is 580 pixels wide. That's narrow enough to be readable without horizontal scrolling for most email clients. Obviously some mobile readers will struggle, but since our main goal is to promote the product of the month, and we want to use a big photo, we can't go too much smaller.

When you're designing for your own client, you may be able to use a flexible column width, but remember to consider your goals and prepare to accommodate different content.

The layout for the body content is fairly simple—essentially a two-column structure, but with a least one section that spans across the full width for the product promo.

We already know that CSS floats won't work, so to build this layout we're going to use tables to hold the content. To ensure that we can put a background color and image (at least for some email clients) in place, we start with a 100% width container table:

modern_henchman_template.html *(excerpt)*

```
<table width="100%" cellspacing="10" cellpadding="0">
</table>
```

Whitespace

I mentioned earlier that several email clients can be sensitive to whitespace in your HTML. In the examples that follow, I've laid out the markup for maximum readability, and it still works well in the clients I've tested. However, this can be unreliable, so if you are adapting this template and run into any weird spacing issues, you should try removing the whitespace to see if that helps.

Inside that is our main content container with a fixed width of 580 pixels:

modern_henchman_template.html *(excerpt)*

```
<table class="main" width="580" cellspacing="0" cellpadding="0"
➥border="0">
```

You'll notice that we're using HTML attributes rather than CSS here for the best results. Nesting tables gives a more reliable layout than we could otherwise achieve, especially with email clients like Outlook and Lotus Notes.

When you're building your own templates, it's a good idea to test in Outlook 2007 (if you can) and Gmail as you progress, so that you find any major layout problems early—these two clients are both common and frequent causes of problems.

Fill the table cells with a block color and add some CSS borders so you can see how the layout is holding together as you work on it.

Adding the Content

Handling the full-width masthead and introduction section is straightforward—they can be added as simple full-width rows to the content table:

modern_henchman_template.html *(excerpt)*

```
<tr>
  <td class="blackbar">
    <table width="100%" border="0" cellspacing="0" cellpadding="0">
      <tr>
        <td align="left" valign="middle" class="left">
          <p>You are receiving this email … </p>
        </td>
      </tr>
    </table>
  </td>
</tr>
<tr>
  <td height="115" align="left" valign="top">
    <table width="580" border="0" cellspacing="0"
        cellpadding="0">
      <tr>
        <td width="290" align="left" valign="top" class="logo">
          <h1>Modern</h1>
          <h1><strong>Henchman</strong></h1>
        </td>
        <td width="290" align="right" valign="top" class="issue">
          <p><strong>In this issue:</strong></p>
          <p>Contents listing</p>
        </td>
      </tr>
    </table>
  </td>
</tr>
<tr>
  <td class="blackbar">
    <table width="100%" border="0" cellspacing="0"
        cellpadding="0">
      <tr>
        <td align="left" valign="middle" class="left">
          <p>Month Name Newsletter</p>
        </td>
        <td class="right" align="right" valign="middle">
          <p>Send to a henchmate | Unsubscribe | … </p>
        </td>
      </tr>
```
⋮

Below that, the two-column layout begins. This looks like a job for yet another table. Nesting another table lets us create consistent padding and margins around the body copy:

modern_henchman_template.html *(excerpt)*

```html
<tr bgcolor="#FFFFFF">
  <td align="center" class="dotsHoriz">
    <table cellspacing="0" cellpadding="0">
      <tr align="left" rowspan="3" valign="top">
        <td width="15" align="left" valign="top" bgcolor="#e6d9d2">
          <p> </p>
        </td>
        <td width="330" align="left" valign="top" bgcolor="#e6d9d2"
            class="mainbar">
          <p>Article photo</p>
          <h2>Article title</h2>
          <p>Article copy</p>
          <p>Read more link</p></td>
        <td width="15" align="left" valign="top" bgcolor="#e6d9d2"
            class="dotsVert">
          <p> </p>
        </td>
        <td width="15" bgcolor="#FFFFFF">
          <p> </p>
        </td>
        <td width="190" align="left" valign="top" bgcolor="#FFFFFF">
          <p>Article photo</p>
          <h3>Article title</h3>
          <p>Article copy</p>
          <p>Read more link</p></td>
        <td width="15" bgcolor="#FFFFFF">
          <p> </p>
        </td>
      </tr>
    </table>
  </td>
</tr>
```

This looks more complicated than it is. We create the two columns, again setting explicit widths. As I've mentioned before, letting the email clients try to work out how wide an element should be is never a good idea, as the results will vary widely.

The secret to this so-called "two-column" layout is actually more columns, hiding around both sides of the content to create the gutter and margins.

Figure 4.5 shows the content block with borders turned on. I have used the Web Developer Toolbar[14] extension for Firefox to display a border around all table cells, which makes it easier to understand what's going on. If you've never worked with table-based layouts before, or have banished them from your mind, this extension can help you make sense of them as you develop your email templates.

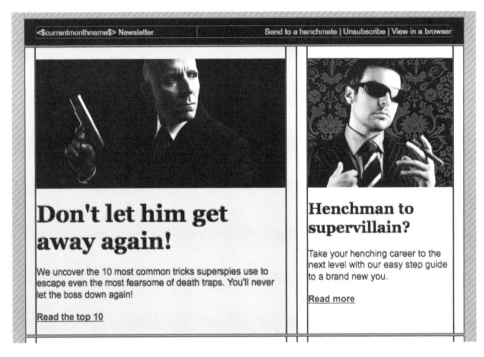

Figure 4.5. The content block with table cells outlined

As you can see, we're using a total of six columns for our two-column layout. I know, it's ugly and old-school, and makes you feel a little bit ill just to look at it. We all feel that way the first time we go back to table layouts.

The nausea will pass eventually, and you'll be left with a two-column layout that displays reliably in all the major email clients. The code for the full-width content

---

[14] https://addons.mozilla.org/en-US/firefox/addon/60

block is very similar, except that it uses only three columns: one for each gutter and one for the content area.

When you need to split a content area further, all you need to do is nest another table. In our example, the "Send to a friend" and "Unsubscribe" blocks at the bottom of the email require nesting another one-column table, like this:

modern_henchman_template.html *(excerpt)*

```
<td class="sidebar" align="left" bgcolor="#ffffff"
    valign="top" width="190">
  <table border="0" cellpadding="0" cellspacing="0" width="100%">
    <tbody>
      <tr>
        <td class="dotsHoriz" align="left" bgcolor="#ffffff"
            height="180" valign="top">
          <h3><img src="images/forward.gif" alt="" align="left"
              height="38" width="40">Send to<br>a henchmate</h3>
          <p>Do your henching colleagues need some tips? … </p>
        </td>
      </tr>
      <tr>
        <td align="left" bgcolor="#ffffff" valign="top">
          <h3><img src="images/unsubscribe.gif" alt="" align="left"
              height="40" width="40">Unsubscribe</h3>
          <p>If you're not interested in being … </p>
        </td>
      </tr>
    </tbody>
  </table>
</td>
```

The complete layout is depicted in Figure 4.6.

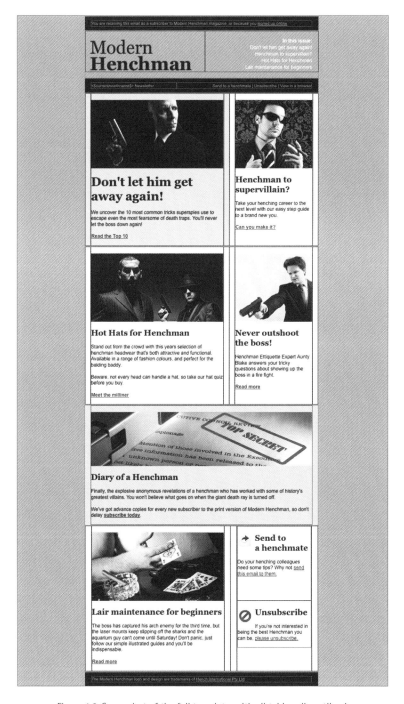

Figure 4.6. Screenshot of the full template, with all table cells outlined

How Low Will You Go?

In building any HTML email template, you'll reach a decision point. Given that the columns are in place, and will hold together well for almost everyone, we could stop pandering to email clients at this point.

If you and your client are okay with some minor visual variation between email clients, you could revert to more modern techniques for the actual content. Just fill in the headings and paragraphs, style them in your CSS, and let them be rendered according to the email client's own quirks.

Most of the time your readers are not going to be comparing the email in different programs, so unless something is really broken they'll be oblivious to minor differences. This is what I'd suggest most of the time, although of course there's still plenty of testing to be done.

If your client is more demanding, or the design really needs to be consistent, you can continue on with further nested tables for individual content chunks. That way you'll have a lot more control over spacing around headings, for example, and control over consistency to let you line up elements with each other.

Here's an example of the effort required to create a consistent heading block:

```
<table cellspacing="0" cellpadding="4" bgcolor="#000000">
  <tbody>
    <tr>
      <td>
        <h2>The actual heading</h2>
      </td>
    </tr>
  </tbody>
</table>
```

This is all the code required just to make sure that the <h2> is displayed at the same size, and with the same surrounding space across the big email clients.

Think carefully before you go to these lengths, because it may well be a waste of your time. It's still good to know that it can be done.

Testing the *Modern Henchman* Layout

Figure 4.7 and Figure 4.8 illustrate how our sample edition of the *Modern Henchman* newsletter looks in a few common email clients. These screenshots were generated using the Campaign Monitor testing tool, but you can achieve similar results from other services.

Figure 4.7. Screenshots in Gmail (left), Windows Live (center), and AOL Desktop 9 (right)

Figure 4.8. Screenshots in Outlook 2007 (left), Thunderbird (center), and Lotus Notes 6.5 (right)

It might be difficult to make out in the screenshots, but there's still some variation from client to client. What you can see is that the overall design is quite close, and certainly doesn't look broken in any of these clients (even though one of the images has failed to load in Lotus Notes 6.5).

The lesson you take away from this should be that you don't need to use only images to achieve consistent results with HTML email. Coding your emails the way I've outlined might require a bit more effort up front, but they will be more effective, so you'll reap rewards in the long run.

More Resources for Building Email Templates

The Web is chock-full of design galleries, and CSS galleries seem to be sprouting up like mushrooms in every corner of it, but there are relatively few HTML email template galleries.

Keep these sites bookmarked for the next design you need to code up, because you can save a ton of time:

- free templates from Campaign Monitor[15]
- ThemeForest templates[16]
- free templates from MailChimp[17]

There's no shame in taking a template that's freely available and has been tested, and adapting it to your needs.

Your client has no interest in paying you to fight a battle to the death with Lotus Notes 7; they just want an email that people can read and that achieves their goals.

Over time you'll build up your own knowledge and a set of working code that you can reuse, which will save you time that's better spent on the design and business goals.

In Chapter 5, we'll step back from the code and take a look at email permission, and our responsibilities as designers.

---

[15] http://www.campaignmonitor.com/templates
[16] http://themeforest.net/category/email-templates
[17] http://www.mailchimp.com/resources/html_email_templates/

Chapter **5**

Understanding Permission

So far we have focused solely on *creating* HTML emails. By now you have all the information you need to be able to think through a design and then build it into a working template.

In this chapter we will be taking a broader look at the business side of commercial email, to understand what should and should not be sent, and who should be receiving it.

Why Designers Should Care about Permission

You might think that managing permission is outside your job description, that you can just do the design and hand it over to your client. In some situations, that may well be true. But even so, there's a huge need for designers to understand the legal, practical, and ethical issues around email marketing.

Why should you care? Pragmatically, if you offer email newsletters as a service to your clients or your employer, you should be able to explain the laws, limits, and best practices of the industry. It will prevent them from running into problems, thereby making your advice and services more valuable.

On a personal level, we should all care about permission because we all receive commercial emails, and not always by choice. Too many people send unwanted email with the help of designers who never bothered to check who the subscribers were going to be.

Finally, you need to know about permission so that you stay on the right side of the law and avoid any legal problems. So, now that I've convinced you of the need to care about permission, let's ask an even more fundamental question: what is permission anyway?

Spam: It's Not Just Viagra

My first rule of spam is that any email that contains the phrase "this is not spam" is almost always spam. My second rule of spam is that nobody thinks that what they're sending is spam.

Of course, this is a massive oversimplification. Obviously some people really are unrepentant spammers who know exactly what they're doing, but many more senders are convinced that what they're doing is not spam, while their recipients think otherwise.

As designers, we obviously need to avoid sending emails that are considered spam by the law. But it's an often-ignored fact that we should also avoid sending emails that are *perceived* as spam. We'll look into that in a moment, but first we'll start with the broadest and most widely accepted definitions of what constitutes spam: the legal definitions. In fact, there's a whole slew of legal definitions, depending on where you're based. The most well-known of these laws, which we touched on in the section called "Legal Compliance" in Chapter 3, is the US CAN-SPAM Act.

Spam According to the Law

If you're sending email as a US company (or for a US company), you're legally bound to comply with the CAN-SPAM laws. For the full details on your obligations, see http://www.ftc.gov/bcp/edu/pubs/business/ecommerce/bus61.shtm.

Here are the core requirements, directly from the Federal Trade Commission, the principal US consumer protection agency:

Don't use false or misleading header information
The From, Reply To, and other address details should all be valid and accurate for the sender and recipient.

Don't use deceptive subject lines
The subject line should accurately reflect the content of the email.

Identify the message as an advertisement
Don't try to disguise it as a personal email, for example. This law indicates why you sometimes see [ADV] in subject lines.

Tell recipients where you're located
Include a valid, physical postal address for the sender.

Provide a way to opt out
You must include a clear, prominent way to opt out of future email (which can be automated or manual).

Honor opt-out requests promptly
You must give people a way to opt out that's available for at least 30 days after you send them the email, and you must act on a request to opt out within ten business days, for free. An online opt-out must only require sending a single email, or visiting a single page.

Clients are unable give us as designers the sole legal burden of complying with these laws; instead, we're jointly responsible for meeting them.

These are the guidelines as of February 2010, but keep in mind that the FTC has made additional rulings since first issuing the laws, so you need to keep an eye out for any future updates.

Many countries have published their own laws regarding spam and commercial email.[1]

---

[1] For a list of relevant laws, see http://www.email-marketing-reports.com/canspam/.

Wherever you live, you need to know the legal issues for you and your clients or company. However, complying with the law is just part of the equation; there are other issues with which to contend.

Permission versus Spam

What the law considers to be spam is often quite distinct (and much narrower) than what the typical email reader considers spam. As a consequence, what an ISP or an email service provider considers spam will often include a lot more than what the laws cover.

Jason Fried and David Heinemeier Hansson of the opinionated web application firm 37signals make this point in *Rework* (New York: Crown Business, 2010):

> Spam is a way of thinking. It's an impersonal, imprecise, inexact approach. You're merely throwing something against the wall to see if it sticks. You're harassing thousands of people hoping that a couple will respond. Press releases are spam. Each one is a generic pitch for coverage sent out to hundreds of journalists you don't know hoping that one will write about you. Resumés are spam when someone shotguns out hundreds at a time to potential employers. They don't care about landing your job, they just care about landing any job. Spam is basically a half-ass way of getting someone's attention. It's insulting, really.

Legally speaking, press releases and resumés are not spam, but the authors of the book consider those kinds of email to be just as spammy as Viagra or mail-order bridal offers. This is a redefinition of spam to extend beyond emails I didn't ask for to also include emails that are irrelevant or worthless.

A 2008 survey by Q Interactive and MarketingSherpa[2] has confirmed that this is a growing definition for individuals as well:

---

[2] http://www.qinteractive.com/newsSingle.asp?nId=227

Underscoring consumers' varying definitions of spam, respondents cited a variety of non-permission-based reasons for hitting the spam button, including "the email was not of interest to me" (41 percent), "I receive too much email from the sender" (25 percent), and "I receive too much email from all senders" (20 percent).

From an email sender's perspective, this can seem unfair. You gather permission according to all the relevant laws, but are still labeled a spammer. Features like the Hotmail unsubscribe button can make it easier for people to achieve the result they want (less email) without having to accuse a sender of spamming; until this type of feature becomes more common, though, the spam button will continue to serve as a proxy for "I don't want your emails."

Email providers and ISPs have publicly admitted to using the same kind of judgment in deciding what counts as email abuse:

> Operationally, we define spam as whatever consumers don't want in their inbox.
> —Yahoo Mail (Miles Libbey, anti-spam product manager)

> I don't care if they've triple opted-in and [given] you their credit card number ... relevance rules, and catering to end user preferences is top priority.
> —AOL (Charles Stiles, AOL Postmaster)

> We need to think really a step beyond opt-in and focus on the consumer's expectations, relevancy, and frequency.
> —Microsoft/Hotmail (Craig Spiezle, online safety evangelist)

> Sometimes people are afraid to report a message because they aren't sure if it is "really" spam or not. Our opinion is that if you didn't ask for it and you don't want it, it's spam to you, and it should be reported.
> —Gmail (Brad Taylor, Google engineer)

The Rise of Relevance

You need more than just permission; you also need to put yourself in your subscribers' shoes. They signed up for information about one of your products, but does that mean they want to be emailed about your other products? Not necessarily.

You've worked with your client or team to determine that you can legally send to subscribers, but there's still work to do. Now you're into the gray area of interest, relevance, and potentially "stale" permission.

There's no way to guarantee that someone, somewhere won't consider any particular email to be spam. In fact, those in the tech industry are the most likely to make blanket statements about all marketing emails being spam, or even all HTML emails.

It's just impossible to make everyone happy, especially those who somehow believe that banning HTML would eradicate spam (instead of creating more plain text spam, which is what would happen). So, what to do?

The best way to avoid being blocked, deleted, flagged, junked, or just plain ignored is to work very hard at making your emails relevant, usable, and useful. That means providing the information you promised when people signed up, and not taking the permission granted for one type of information and stretching it out to cover other topics.

Practically, this means being clear about why people should sign up, and then providing those benefits consistently. As designers, we can take this all the way from the initial sign-up form. Compare the two sign-up forms shown in Figure 5.1 and Figure 5.2.

RECEIVE OUR NEWSLETTER

ENTER EMAIL ADDRESS   SUBSCRIBE NOW

Figure 5.1. Generic form

STAY CONNECTED!

Subscribe and receive feature and best practice articles on email marketing, interactive design and online strategy.

ENTER EMAIL ADDRESS   SUBSCRIBE NOW

Figure 5.2. Sign-up form explaining benefits and showing an example issue

Even before any email is sent, each form has created its distinct audience. People who signed up through the first form will be expecting a newsletter, yes, but what will it contain? What will it look like? How frequently will they receive it?

They could be imagining something quite different from what you actually intend to send. If it turns out to be unsatisfactory, they may simply unsubscribe. But they might also mark your email as spam. Subscribers to the second form will be expecting exactly what you intend to send, so they'll know it when they see it, and they're more likely to remember signing up for it.

Designing for relevance carries through to the content. You need to make sure that not only is the actual subject matter relevant, but that the design makes this clear by putting the valuable information up front, rather than burying it in unrelated promotions or cross-selling.

Providing timely and useful information is the best defense against spam complaints, not to mention apathy and indifference. After all, receiving no response at all can be even more disheartening than receiving complaints.

Understanding Spam Complaints

Even the cleanest, most permission-based of lists will probably result in a complaint or two eventually. Not every complaint is legitimate—some are accidentally triggered, and others are from readers who think that hitting "mark as spam" is the easiest way to unsubscribe. As we saw in the section called "Permission versus Spam", many email software companies are actively encouraging this kind of behavior, so you need to know what it means and how to react.

Spam complaints come in a few forms, so knowing what they all are helps when trying to avoid them (as well as when dealing with the ones that are impossible to avoid).

Direct Complaints

Direct complaints are when a subscriber actively sends an email that says, literally, "This is spam" or calls on the phone. The complaint might come directly to you or to your client, or to your email service provider, or even to the ISP that provides bandwidth for the servers that send the emails.

Feedback Loops

Some ISPs and email providers (Comcast and Hotmail are two examples) have special systems set up that can collect complaints from their users and forward them on in a specific format to the email service provider that send the emails.

The service provider then receives those complaints and processes them according to its company policy. In the case of Campaign Monitor, the recipient is automatically unsubscribed, and a record is added to the sender's campaign report showing that a complaint was made. This is fairly typical of the way feedback loop complaints are handled.

Feedback loops are almost always triggered by direct action (that is, a reader clicking a "Mark as spam" button or similar) rather than by an automated filter process. So the end result is much the same as a direct complaint, except that it can more easily be acted on, since it's in a format that can be actioned by an automated software process.

If you choose to use an email service provider, you can check with them as to whether they're integrated with feedback loops. While it might seem risky to open yourself up to such direct complaints, it's better to handle them right away than find out that you've been blacklisted later on.[3]

---

[3] You can find a list of the major feedback loops at http://blog.deliverability.com/feedback.html.

Automated Filtering

Some email systems will generate warnings and complaints when they detect a certain volume or frequency of emails that are considered possible spam. Generally those will be sent to your email service provider rather than directly to you as the sender, but your email service provider would then follow up with you.

What to Do with Spam Complaints

In all cases, being able to show how permission was obtained for any particular subscriber is critical. A fast, detailed response to a complaint that provides permission details and offers to unsubscribe the address will usually avoid any ongoing problems.

Clients often feel understandably defensive about their lists and can be tempted to respond aggressively, but it's important to make them understand that this kind of response is counterproductive. Although some complaints may well be unfair, email providers have to take each one seriously, so it pays to be prepared with evidence of an email list that's fully permission-based.

Keeping a record of who has complained is essential, in order to avoid emailing them again. Some email systems will do this for you, and you should find out if that's the case for your provider.

Above all, spam complaints are valuable feedback and should be accepted as your recipients letting you know something about your list. By reading their minds a little, we can interpret a simple spam complaint in different ways:

"I don't remember signing up for this."

How long ago did the people on your list sign up? It could be that the span of time between signing up and receiving an email was too long, or that the sign-up form was unclear about how frequent the emails would be.

"I did not agree to these emails."

Was the opt-in process very clear? A common cause of complaints is forcing people to join your list as part of entering a competition. Both the sign-up form and the emails themselves need to be extremely clear about what's happening.

If a reader signed up to win a prize, but the first email makes no mention of the competition at all, they're much more likely to consider it spam.

"This is not useful information."
Perhaps the content of the email isn't what was promised. Don't promise useful hints and tips and then send promotional junk every month.

"I don't care about this anymore."
Maybe the reader just moved on and no longer has a need for your product or service. The spam complaint might mean they don't want to receive your emails anymore and thought hitting "Mark as spam" was the best way to achieve it.

"I can't be bothered to unsubscribe."
Related to the previous point. As I've already mentioned, making the unsubscribe link hard to find is self-defeating. If your reader doesn't want any more emails, don't try to trick them into staying on your list. Put a simple and clear unsubscribe link right up front, and avoid forcing people to complain.

Any email newsletter service you use will have their own spam complaint process, which you'll need to know about and explain to clients. Most people never run into serious complaints, but it can happen and you do need to be prepared.

How many complaints is too many?

There isn't any one number that you can rely on. Every email service will have their own "safe" level, but even one complaint can cause problems if it reveals that permission was not obtained properly.

In practice, there's always a "normal" level of complaints, appearing like background radiation no matter what you do. That number is typically very low, around 0.01%. If your campaigns are receiving complaints at around that frequency, there's no need to be too concerned.

Obviously, if you're dealing with very small lists one complaint can be a big percentage, so in order to gain an accurate view you'll need to average it out over a number of campaigns.

Again, check with the system you use to email, or with your ISP, as to what they consider to be a bad number of complaints.

How can I know if my client has permission?

When you're sending your own campaigns, you have all the information you need to know whether your list is permission-based, and what kind of emails the people on the list will be expecting. When it comes to dealing with clients, however, it can be a little bit trickier.

You can ask them to read the permission rules that apply for your chosen email service, but how can you know if they're giving you all the information? There are a few guidelines for exploring how permission was obtained that should help avoid unpleasant surprises after sending.

Ask for Details

Don't settle for a simple "yes, this list is fine." Ask more detailed questions, such as "Can you give me a list of the different ways people can make it onto this list, like forms on your website, or signing up in person or by email?"

This will make your client think in more depth about how the list was constructed, and may bring up some new information.

Restate Their Permission Answer and Ask for Confirmation

If you've asked your client whether they followed all the relevant guidelines, and they say that they have but you're still concerned, seek a direct confirmation.

"Just to confirm, all 955 of these people signed up on your website. You didn't add anyone at all?" If they've any doubts or have forgotten other ways, this could help them remember.

Compare the Explanation Given to the Email Content

See if the email content makes sense in the context of how the list was supposedly gathered. If your client is telling you that their list is made up customers who've recently bought a certain product, but their email copy directly promotes that same product, that's a sign you should ask a few more questions.

Explain Why it Matters

Most people think that their entire subscriber list will be ecstatic to hear from them. Clients often won't realize that there are risks for them in sending to a list that isn't permission-based. If they receive spam complaints, but they do have explicit permission from each person they emailed, then it can be resolved. On the other hand, if they receive complaints from people who fall outside the legal or commercial criteria for having given permission, their account could be closed or they could be blacklisted.

Going through this process with your clients can be annoying, but it will protect their reputation—and also your own—if complaints do start to come in. If your client is sending from their own servers or from a dedicated IP address, blacklists are also a concern.

Blacklists, Whitelists, and Sender Reputation

Due to years of abuse from deliberate spammers, hundreds of services have popped up to deal with this problem. If you're using an external provider, they'll generally take care of ensuring that their emails bypass these anti-spam services.

If you're using your own servers, your client's servers, or a dedicated external server, the task will fall to your client and their consultants to handle it. Such details fall outside the scope of this book, but having a good understanding of what blacklists are and how they work will help with planning and implementing your email campaigns.

Blacklists

In the email world, a **blacklist** (also called DNSBL for DNS Based Black List) is a list of IP addresses that are linked in some way to spam. Anti-spam software and mail servers can refer to this list of addresses when receiving mail, to decide whether to allow it to be delivered. Blacklists can form a part, or the whole, of the process of filtering an email.

If the server you use to send email is listed on a major blacklist, your emails may be more heavily filtered, or be blocked altogether. A major part of an email service provider's value is in monitoring these lists and making sure that their IP addresses remain off blacklists.

Inevitably, legitimate servers will be listed (perhaps because of inaccurate complaints), but a good email service will follow up and usually be delisted fairly quickly. If your client wants to handle sending the emails themselves, or wants you to handle it, you should make them aware of the amount of work that can be involved in managing this part of the equation.

To find out if a particular IP address is listed, you can go directly to a specific list provider. Alternatively, you can use one of the aggregator tools, such as DNSBL.info,[4] and enter the IP address there.

Whitelists

Where a blacklist works by letting all email past except for mail from specific IPs, a **whitelist** takes the opposite approach and blocks everything by default. Only email from a specified set of IP addresses is allowed past.

Historically, some of the large email providers did have systems for whitelisting known senders, but this approach is becoming increasingly rare as they move to reputation-based systems that measure complaints, volume of sends, bounces, and the like. If your client is having problems reaching a particular domain, especially if it belongs to a smaller company, requesting to be added to the domain's whitelist can often resolve the problem.

Overall, this kind of list-based spam system is only a small part of the email game. If we all concentrate on sending relevant, useful information that people have actually requested, we'll be in the best position to have our emails delivered in the long term.

---

[4] http://www.dnsbl.info/dnsbl-database-check.php

Sender Reputation

While both blacklists and whitelists are declining in relevance and importance, **sender reputation** is rapidly becoming the key way of ensuring emails are delivered. Organizations like Return Path[5] provide a service that ranks email senders according to a combination of metrics mixed into a single score that represents the reputation of the sender.

Email administrators and providers can use that rating in their filtering when deciding if an email is legitimate. According to Ken Takahashi of Return Path, the following elements make up a sender reputation:

- the volume of email you send (and how consistent that volume is)

- the number and percentage of bounces your emails receive

- the rate of complaints

- whether you're emailing known **spam trap** addresses (email addresses specifically set up just to catch spam, and never opted into or signed up for anything)

- longevity of business (how long you've been sending)

- infrastructure (whether you have all the capabilities to handle authentication, bounces, unsubscribes, and the like)

Looking at this list, it's clear that a quality email service provider is well worth the cost, as there's a lot of work in maintaining a system that deals with all those areas.[6]

---

[5] http://www.returnpath.net/
[6] A great resource for understanding how sender reputation impacts on deliverability and permission can be found at http://www.email-marketing-reports.com/deliverability/.

Understanding Authentication

In this chapter, we've used the word "permission" to refer to an individual opting in to receive emails from a person or business. There's also another definition of permission in email, and that is at the mail server level.

Authentication is a way for a domain owner to say, "I give my permission for emails to be sent on my behalf by this mail server."

Because of the way email was originally built, it's difficult to prove that an email is actually coming from the person who claims to be sending it. Email authentication fixes this by letting you add some simple information to your domain's DNS records that define who's allowed to send email on your behalf.

Without going into too much detail, there are two main authentication standards: Sender ID and DomainKeys/DKIM. Different ISPs use either or a combination of both, so to achieve the best results you would want to implement them both.

All the large ISPs like AOL, Hotmail, Yahoo, and Gmail are using email authentication as an important layer in deciding whether to allow an email to be delivered. By using authentication, you can instantly bypass some filters, giving your campaigns a better chance of arriving in the destination inbox.

Not only that, but many ISPs, such as Yahoo and Hotmail, will visually flag your email as authenticated, which helps to build trust between you and your subscribers, improving the chances of your emails being opened. To implement it, you'll need access to the DNS for the sending domain, so it's unfeasible if you want to apply it to your client's hotmail.com address. For a corporate domain, adding authentication records (normally given to you by your email service provider) is a great idea.

As of 2010, your email should still be delivered even if you are not using authentication, but there are signs that this could happen down the road, so it's worth investigating now.

Permission and the Future of Email

We've gone through a whole chapter and barely once mentioned HTML or CSS, but understanding permission is just as important as your ability to design and build emails.

Every time you take on a new HTML email design job, you need to understand who the audience is, how they agreed to receive the email, and what benefit they'll derive from it. Avoid the temptation of leaving it until the last minute, because the consequences can be widespread and quite serious.

Chapter

6

Selling Email to Your Clients

You've spent time understanding the legalities of email, and learning the technicalities of creating HTML email that looks great across all of the most common email clients. Now it's time to gain a return on the time you've already invested in email!

Selling email services is a logical step forward for freelance web designers and developers. This chapter will look at the practicalities of selling email to existing and new clients. Once we review the reasons you should add email to your service offering, we'll take a closer look at the variety of email-related services that you can offer, and what is involved in selling email services. We will cover the common approaches to pricing and preparing a folio of email samples, and discuss tips for a winning client pitch.

Why Sell Email Services?

We've spent the last five chapters of this book discussing HTML email from every perspective. So perhaps this section would be more appropriately titled, "Why *wouldn't* you sell email services?"

More than Just a Designer or Developer ...

If you see yourself purely as a web designer or developer, it's time to broaden that view. The first important step in selling your email services is to recognize your capabilities in email design and delivery. Then you'll be able to see—and present—yourself as someone who designs or develops more than websites alone.

There's one particularly good reason why you should sell email services. If you're freelancing, email services provide a prime opportunity to maintain ongoing, potentially lucrative relationships with clients. Designers and developers often find that they have few reasons to continue the client relationship once they've delivered the site they were contracted to provide. Email is a very handy solution to the challenge of maintaining close client relationships over time.

A client who's just paid good money to have a website developed will usually be quick to grasp the potential that email marketing offers, and they'll want to make the most of it. As we know, email is an established, widely used online marketing tool that's readily embraced by users: according to a MarketingSherpa report from 2010,[1] 65% of all email users felt that email was the best way for companies to communicate with them. As stated back in the section called "Email: The Heart of the Internet" in Chapter 1, it's also extremely measurable and cost-effective. For clients who are focused on brand—and revenue—building online, email will usually be a logical, and, indeed, essential part of the plan. And who better than you, their trusted web designer or developer, to provide that service?

Similarly, email services can be a good way to get your foot in the door of organizations for which you'd like to do more work. Approach a prospect who you know doesn't currently use email to communicate with industry or client contacts, secure a contract to design and deliver a new email newsletter or catalog, and you might have the beginnings of a great—and growing—business relationship.

In any case, the benefits of a recurring revenue that results from an ongoing contract for email services are evident. If you've been looking to provide add-on services that will give you a reliable bread-and-butter income each month, email offerings are an excellent place to start.

---

[1] http://www.marketingsherpa.com/article.php?ident=31519

What Can You Sell?

So, you want to sell email services. What exactly does that mean?

 Identify Your Expertise

Before you try to work out what you can sell, it's important to recognize the difference between selling technical services and selling marketing services. For those of us who've spent our careers designing and building websites, it may seem quite a leap to shift from that skill set to selling email services. What if the client wants advice on audience segmentation, content strategy, or some other marketing-related aspect of email?

Perhaps you already have experience in email marketing, so you're comfortable with responding to client questions on these topics. On the other hand, you may prefer to restrict your offering to the purely technical: design, testing, delivery, list management, and tracking. Whatever the case, now is a good time to start thinking about these issues and identifying the areas in which you feel you can best help your clients.

In this section, we'll stick specifically to the technical aspects of the email services you might sell. If you want to move beyond these to sell email marketing services, SitePoint's *The Email Marketing Kit* (Melbourne: SitePoint, 2007), by Jeanne S. Jennings, has all the advice you'll need.

If you're a freelancer, it's likely you've already identified the essential skills you'll be able to sell to clients:

Email template design

We talked about designing email in Chapter 3, and developing a robust email template in Chapter 4; these are obviously saleable skills. You might also choose to package landing page design with this service for cases where the client's running a campaign that needs specific functionality or a particular sales focus. If your client is requesting a template for a regular email newsletter, you can also include the design of the subscription page.

Email management system development

Some clients will be happy to manage their emails through a third-party web-based system. If you're a developer, however, you may be able to create your own and provide a full proprietary email solution—from list management to template design—to clients who want to administer their own email subscription lists and communications securely on their own system.

Email delivery

Despite the wealth of usable email marketing tools out there, many clients are hesitant to take responsibility for inputting and sending emails themselves. If you're happy to drop the template you've developed into your own, or a web-based, email service, prepare the mailing list, and hit the Send button, those clients may be happy to pay you for your help.

List management

Remember the legal pitfalls we discussed in Chapter 5? It's no surprise that many site managers would prefer to hand responsibility for the management of email lists, subscriptions, and unsubscribes to a skilled professional like you. If your client wants to merge two databases into one, they may need you to wash the databases against one another to remove problem addresses (invalid and dummy addresses, for example) from the mix, as well as ensure that individuals who've signed up to both lists are included in the merged subscriber list only once.

Campaign review and consultation

We're straying into email marketing territory here, but even if you decide you'll only provide technical services, you may be able to recommend layout or design tweaks that might boost subscription rates, increase open rates, or reduce opt-outs for your clients. You might also provide A/B testing facilities (including design, delivery, and review) for clients who want to hone their email marketing efforts.

Within these broad categories, you may be able to think of a number of offerings to interest existing or prospective customers. The way you integrate these offerings will depend on your clients, your level of interest, and how you choose to package your services.

As an example, you might decide to offer a full email newsletter service that includes the following features:

- the design of subscription forms and a subscription page for the client's site

- the design of email templates to be sent via an autoresponder to sign up customers successfully

- the design of an email newsletter template

- A/B testing of two separate newsletter executions to work out which is the most effective with the client's userbase

- subscription list management, including sign-ups and duplicates, bounces, and unsubscribes handling

- monthly production and mailing of the newsletter using content provided by the client

- the production of a monthly email report showing the total messages sent, delivered, opened, and bounced for each mail-out (you could also provide cumulative reports that show statistical behavior over time)

How to Sell Email Services

Now that you've worked out what you're going to sell, let's think about how you'll sell it.

Selling email services involves three components. The first task is to work out what you'll charge for your offering, and on what basis you'll apply those charges. We'll look at this topic next.

Then, you'll need to work out how to pitch these new services successfully to your clients. In the section called "Preparing Your Pitch" I'll prepare a few items that can help you communicate the possibilities and benefits of email for your clients.

Finally, in the section called "Promoting Email Services to Clients and Prospects" we'll look at the ways you might announce your new email services to existing and prospective clients. We'll also see how you can integrate them seamlessly into your overall service offering.

Pricing Email Marketing Services

When it comes to pricing your services, the world is, effectively, your oyster. Let's look at pricing on the basis of the way you might offer your services: on a per-skill basis, and as a series of package deals.

Pricing Your Skills

If you've decided to sell your services on the basis of skills—template design, delivery, list management, and so on—you're probably looking at two charging options.

The most obvious option is to charge by the hour, but you could charge a flat fee instead; the latter acts as a sort of "easy sell" that stops your less confident or more budget-conscious clients from worrying just how much they'll wind up paying for the service. Table 6.1 lists some of the services we discussed above, and identifies their most common pricing options.

Table 6.1. Services and the Common Charging Options

Service	Charging options
Template design	Hourly rate or flat fee
Creative amendments	Hourly rate or flat fee
Email delivery	Calculated on the basis of list size
Mail-out review and consultation	Hourly rate or flat fee
Database washing	Hourly rate or calculated on the basis of list size
Mail-out report provision	Flat fee
A/B testing and reporting	Hourly rate or flat fee
List management	Hourly rate, flat fee, or calculated on the basis of list size
List and image hosting	Calculated on the basis of file size/storage required

As you can see in Table 6.1, the one area where charging by the hour is less appropriate is where the list size plays a role. Many freelancers base their email delivery service charges on the size of the mail-out, since the costs of the mailing increase as the list grows. The same logic applies to hosting and list management service charges.

It's also important to note that although some of these services—particularly list and image hosting—may be included in a web-based email management service package, many freelancers charge clients separately for them. It's true that these items might fall outside the freelancer's direct action. However, they may see these charges as offsetting related costs that may not be covered by their own client service package price. For example, if they need to liaise with the email service's support team over the hosting of image files, or to obtain backups of client data at some point, there'll be no need to charge the client separately for those hours, since they've already been covered by the hosting price.

In choosing which pricing method to use, you'll probably gravitate toward your current pricing approach. But you should always consider how the client will react. If they're unfamiliar with email marketing and have never collected details for a subscriber list before, a flat fee may put their minds at ease regarding the potential of costs escalating. Alternatively, your existing clients may be curious if you, a staunch by-the-hour designer, suddenly offer services for a flat fee. And if you do opt for flat-fee pricing, keep in mind that some clients will take up more of your time than others.

You might want to set your price at a point that allows for some back and forth with the client, or contains a percentage of "fat" for unexpected discussions or delays. This is especially relevant if you've created a flat-fee structure to convince clients who are inexperienced with email to give it a try. You may need to do extra legwork to keep them comfortable and answer their questions as the development progresses. Be sure to allow some form of extra time in your flat-fee structure.

Ultimately, the answer to the question of pricing really depends on you, your clients, your relationships, and the way you do business. If you'd feel happier charging by the hour for everything, and you can sell this option to current and potential clients, go for it.

Pricing Service Packages

Pricing service packages like the one we discussed in the section called "What Can You Sell?" will obviously require you to work out how much you'll charge for each component of the package first. You may find that when you group tasks into a complete bundle, working on them becomes more of a fluid process than would completing these tasks individually. You also stand to gain economies in the project management aspect of the job, given that you'll be working with one client across the spectrum of tasks. These continuity benefits might allow you to shave an hour off here or there, providing better value than you would if providing the services individually.

But what should you do if a client wants only some of the services on offer? The example we saw in the section called "What Can You Sell?" included A/B testing. But what if, perhaps for reasons of time or budget pressure, your client doesn't want to test their email? Can you remove that service from the package? If so, by how much will that affect the package's price?

If you've reduced your overall package price to account for the benefits that the continuity of the work will bring, you won't want to cut the package price by the original cost you allotted to A/B testing, since that now represents a larger portion of the "optimized" price. In this case, it might be more accurate to reduce the overall package cost by a percentage of that original sum you calculated for A/B testing.

Perhaps you'll develop a standard calculation that allows you to to drop in or pull out components of your service package easily. This will make it easier to establish how much the price will change if a client adds or removes a component from the package, and saves you having to go back to the pricing drawing board every time they decide to add or drop a service.

However you structure your pricing, it's important that you communicate it clearly and transparently to clients. We'll look at these considerations next.

Preparing Your Pitch

In preparing to actually sell your email services to clients and prospects, you'll need more than an idea of what you'll offer and how you'll charge. Your clients may be eager email marketers, or they may have no experience at all in this field. You'll know where your clients sit on this spectrum, and from this point it's a matter of putting together the collateral that will convince them to pay for your email services.

Your Sales Pitch

Whether you prepare a pre-sales whitepaper to introduce prospects to the benefits of email services, or simply spend half an hour discussing the topic with them over a coffee, you need to be able to prove that email marketing delivers.

The Direct Marketing Association's research on the average return on investment for email is available on its site,[2] and its key findings are regularly reported in various news sources. A quick web search will turn up the most current research results, which you can use in your discussions with clients. The same is true for data on email market penetration, its usage by organizations in particular countries, and the acceptance of email marketing by target recipients. This kind of information can make persuasive reading (or listening!) for your prospects. You might even consider creating a quick comparison of how email performs against other marketing tactics to clearly indicate the effectiveness of email.

As well as answering the question, "Why should I use email?", you might need to explain to prospects why they need to pay for email when they can send it from their own computers free of charge. You'll want to show them how easy, flexible, and cost-effective email campaign management can be, and the benefits it delivers. Explain the kinds of headaches prospects can avoid if they use appropriate tools to manage their mailing lists. Step them through the process of setting up a test campaign in your system, using them and yourself as recipients. And highlight the value of the tracking data they can gain through a properly managed campaign, perhaps by showing them examples of tracking reports.

If you've already run a campaign or two for clients (or yourself) you might prepare case examples of those campaigns that identify the clients' objectives, how you met their needs, and what sort of results they obtained in a given time frame. Be sure to obtain permission to mention the names of the clients to which you've provided email services—it's sure to encourage your prospects to start wondering if they'll be left behind if they bypass email marketing.

---

[2] http://www.the-dma.org/

Lacking any real-life email campaign results?

If you don't have any results of actual campaigns that are suitable to use as case studies, you might be able to compile that information in other ways:

- Ask a peer or associate if they can provide you with some live, anonymous data to use in your sales kit.

- Run a few campaigns of your own for side projects you have on the go, and use that information to create reports that prove how easy it is to monitor email campaigns.

- Search for such case studies online or in relevant print publications. Educational email marketing materials often detail real-life campaigns and explain how and why they were successful.

Finally, compile electronic and printed examples of different email types so that your prospects can gain a clear idea of which formats might work for them. Consider also preparing a schedule of rates for your email services or packages so they can see at a glance what kind of money they need to spend to reach a given audience size.

Your Email Service Folio

A email service folio is an excellent sales tool, as it provides visual proof that you can create what you promise. Even if you're just starting out in this field, and you have no working email examples, you might create samples of the different email types to show prospects. A collection of carefully honed examples will indicate even to the least creative of your prospects what you can do for them.

Your Name Here!

While you're preparing different email examples, why not tailor them specifically to your prospects? You could include their logo and brand name in the design, and reflect their products, services, and clientele in the content. As well as attention-grabbing, this tactic can help your prospects establish a connection between their brand and email marketing.

If you have real campaign data, marry the creative examples with brief fact sheets that identify the response rates generated, and the return the clients gained on their investments. This information will go a long way to convincing prospects that you know what you're doing. Not only does it show that you're focused on the business benefits of email, it also proves that you can help them achieve real results.

Presenting your folio online, along with case information, testimonials, and results data wherever you can is undoubtedly your best option for presenting your email service capabilities. Once you've completed email projects for a few clients, you might like to present a case study for each of the services or packages you offer. In the meantime, publish examples of your creative output to show off your capabilities in email marketing.

Promoting Email Services to Clients and Prospects

So you've prepared your sales materials, and you're ready to start selling email services. Great! But how can you promote those services to your clients? Should you just give them a call and set up a meeting to discuss the topic? Or try to slip email services casually into your next conversation?

Your sales approach will depend on your clients and your own personal style. Here are a few tactics you might consider for communicating your new service to clients:

Start your own email newsletter

If you're yet to do so already, create an email newsletter that you can send regularly to clients. You might use it to keep them updated on your service offering and additions to your online folio, point them to research that may help them use their website to its full potential, or provide them with web tips and hints. A well-planned and executed email newsletter can be a good way to practice what, effectively, you're trying to preach. It'll also give you some folio pieces and live mailing statistics that you can use in sales pitches.

Add the new service offering to your website

Remember to add information about your email services to your website. Potential clients who visit the site will then be aware of your full service offering, which is likely to push you higher up their shortlist of potential providers.

Approach existing clients

Go through your current client list and identify the businesses you believe will particularly benefit from your new services. Contact the appropriate people to set up a meeting so you can explain how email might fit into their marketing and online strategies. If you've prepared a whitepaper or article about the benefits of email, you might opt to send it through to them before the meeting. Finally, tailor a pitch that includes a specialized email sample with their brand and business, plus clear recommendations about the ways in which email might help them achieve their goals, and which of your services you believe will best benefit them.

Approach new clients

You may use your new services as a basis to target prospects who you haven't worked with before. If you can see an opportunity for email in a given organization, you might find others in the same industry that are yet to embrace the benefits of email. You may use some of the more traditional promotional means—printing postcards, writing articles on email's relevance and benefits for industry publications, attending local networking events, and so on—to reach these new clients. If you have a promotional budget, you may also try some email marketing of your own: create a targeted campaign to send to a qualified contact list that you've purchased from a reputable broker.

Build email services into your brand

You may think that adding your new service listing to your website and placing examples of your work in your folio is all you need to do to make email part of your repertoire. But these tactics are just the start—you can go much further. Consider:

- commenting on email marketing research, news and developments, the campaigns you're working on, and the success of email as a communications medium through the social networking tools you use

- building email into every pitch you make to a client

- adding an "Email services" item to your website's main navigation or your organization's tag line making email integral to your own business's communications, to build your brand, communicate with your audiences, and promote your offerings

You may wish to avoid diluting the strong brand you've built by becoming "the email person" overnight. Despite this, focusing strongly on email can help establish it as a key part of your service offering, especially in the early stages. Be creative in your search for promotional opportunities. Perhaps you'll put up your hand to mail match schedules and results to members of your soccer club, and maintain the subscriber email database. Design an eye-catching template on an otherwise quiet afternoon, and you may well impress some friends who want to use email in their businesses, or who know someone who could!

Conclusion

You've worked hard to develop skills in designing, coding, and distributing HTML email. It makes sense to put a price on those skills and sell them.

We began this chapter by asking "Why sell email services?" Well, why *wouldn't* you? We discussed shifting your mindset so that you no longer see yourself as purely a web designer or developer. Then we talked about just a few of the reasons you should sell email services—including the fact that, as a logical extension of your offering, email provides an excellent opportunity to maintain ongoing, paying relationships with clients.

Throughout this book, I hope I've been able to show you that HTML email is a powerful tool both you and your clients should be using, and, moreover, that it requires all the same familiar HTML and CSS skills you've been using for years. Now you have everything you need to gain a head start in this market.

You have the skills and the knowledge. It's time to take your email services to the world!

Index